DISCOURSES
OF THE
ELDERS

DISCOURSES
OF THE
ELDERS

The Aztec *Huehuetlatolli*

A First English Translation

Collected by Friar Andrés de Olmos circa 1535

With Supplemental Texts

Introduced and Translated by

SEBASTIAN PURCELL

W. W. NORTON & COMPANY
Independent Publishers Since 1923

To my wife *y mi hija*. To my old man, a crazy hippie who proposed marriage to a *mexicana* in secret, because he knew he'd never receive permission, *y mi madre, la mexicana* who agreed to it.

For information about permission to reproduce selections from this book, write to Permissions, W. W. Norton & Company, Inc., 500 Fifth Avenue, New York, NY 10110

For information about special discounts for bulk purchases, please contact W. W. Norton Special Sales at specialsales@wwnorton.com or 800-233-4830

Manufacturing by Lakeside Book Company
Book design by Chris Welch
Production manager: Louise Mattarelliano

Library of Congress Control Number: 2024936013

ISBN 978-1-324-07616-2 pbk.

W. W. Norton & Company, Inc., 500 Fifth Avenue, New York, N.Y. 10110
www.wwnorton.com

W. W. Norton & Company Ltd., 15 Carlisle Street, London W1D 3BS

1 2 3 4 5 6 7 8 9 0

Contents

PART I
THE DISCOURSES OF THE ELDERS

PART II
SOCIAL ROLE DESCRIPTIONS

Translator's Introduction

This translation has been undertaken and supported by what is perhaps a timely optimism.[1] After too long,[2] professional philosophers in the anglophone world and the European continent seem to be recognizing the existence of other global traditions of philosophy and what contributions they might make. They have also come to recognize the need, if we are to consider ourselves philosophers and not just apologists for the "West,"[3] to reflect seriously on what those traditions might have to contribute. Philosophy is a difficult practice, after all, and one reason for this is that it has never been easy for a person to imagine how things could have been otherwise.[4] How, for example, can one carry on a metaphysical inquiry without making use of "being," either as a word or even as a notion implied through one's grammar? What would it mean for our moral psychology to take seriously the notion that our "mind" is distributed through the organs of our body, and that they compete to direct our attention and decisions? What would it mean to have a virtue of character that, in optimal circumstances, operated by way of shared agency—that is, in groups? What if practical wisdom is conceived collectively rather than individually?

The people whom we call the Aztecs understand our circumstances in just the way these questions suggest. They have a metaphysical tradition, but no concept of "being."[5] They have a sense of "mind," but do not conceive of it as distinct from our body.[6] Moreover, they think of our comprehension and judgment as distributed among the different senses of our body, so that these various centers competed for attention and influence.[7] The Aztecs also have a form of virtue ethics.[8] This is the ethical approach found in Plato and Aristotle and it is taken to deem an action as right when it follows from a virtuous quality of character, such as courage or justice.[9] Unlike that articulation, however, the Aztecs conceive every one of those virtues to function, in the optimal case, by way of shared agency in some capacity. This point was nowhere more accurate than in their understanding of practical wisdom, which they think is best exercised in groups, not by individuals. In opposition to Aristotle's lone *phronimos*, the practically wise man, they urge that we think of the practically wise group.[10]

All these points shift our philosophical imagination. They urge us to reconsider whether the paradigms that "Western" philosophy has been using, whether for metaphysics, epistemology, moral psychology, or ethical theory, have been informed largely by chance and not careful reflection. It is at least worth considering. Perhaps we are wrong about things, even profoundly wrong? We could try to imagine our way out of this possibility through thought experiments, but is it not more reasonable to look to, and reflect on, established traditions of philosophy to do this work?

If both good philosophical method and reasonable optimism about the existence of human intelligence in other cultures urge the study of Aztec philosophy, then there nevertheless remains a real practical objection to its study: almost none of it is accessible to anyone who is not already a specialist. Several of the most important texts from this tradition have never been translated into English. Moreover, what works do exist are scattered across many volumes, often difficult to obtain, with a wide range of accuracy in their rendering. Finally, none of the works that exist in translation, in any language, have been rendered with cognizance of philosophical terms, topics, and interests. It is to address this threefold deficiency that I set out to translate these *Huehuetlatolli*, or *Discourses of the Elders*, which Friar Andrés de Olmos compiled beginning around 1535.

A *huehuetlatolli* (pronounced way-we-tla-TOL-li and sometimes written *huehuehtlahtolli*) is a genre unique to the Nahuatl-speaking peoples of central Mexico just before Hernán Cortés defeated Tenochtitlán's people in 1521. It consists of discourses, *tlahtolli*, from older persons to younger persons. The *huehuetque* were elders. After these long speeches, the younger persons followed with brief replies. It is for this reason that they have been called "dialogues," even though they stand at some distance from that idea.[11] For a philosopher, the topics prove crucial, since they concern the final goals of life and how one should live to achieve them. It is, in short, a uniquely ethical genre. By reading this set of discourses, as a result, the outlines of the Aztec ethical landscape come nicely and naturally into view. And they do so in what is likely the most introductory path available.

At this point, it is worth noting a nuance about names. The indigenous people in question would have called themselves by their cities of origin, not Aztecs. While this is the most widely recognized designation, it proves peculiar, since it names the indigenous people after their mythical place of origin. It would be as if, rather than referring to the Greeks of classical "Western" antiquity as Greeks, we called them "Olympians," because their myths centered on Mt. Olympus. It would be more consistent with our naming practices to call these peoples of Mesoamerica the Nahuas, since they spoke, and later wrote, in Nahuatl. Nevertheless, even this name, Nahua, is largely an artifact of scholarship,[12] since the peoples themselves would have preferred designations such as the Mexica, the Tlaxcalteca, and the like.

The present volume is thus conceived as the first philosophical translation of a core set of Nahua philosophical documents into any modern language and prepared for the nonspecialist. These discourses have not been available to English readers previously, and the reader will need some guideposts before venturing into the work itself, as the Nahua view is sufficiently unfamiliar to our own that the nonspecialist might easily be overwhelmed.

What follows in this introduction is an explanation of the decisions that guided the present translation, the relevant context of the manuscript itself, and an outline of the contents. To begin, it will be helpful to have a sense of the broader Nahua philosophy, or at least the dominant strand of that philosophy which is present in these discourses, so that it may then be easier, later, to explain what aims have guided the present *philosophical* translation. The reader will also more easily find their way through the texts that follow. Let's begin with the basics.

Metaphilosophical Points

My picture of Nahua philosophy, especially their ethics, is notably different from the accounts put forth by anthropologists and historians—but not without reason.

Imagine that humanity is fortunate enough to survive well into the twenty-second century and that two groups of researchers look back on our age to articulate our attitudes toward the environment. The first group is composed of historians and anthropologists who survey all the written statements by environmental advocates, as well as written evidence of the daily practices of regular folk who drove carbon-emitting vehicles to work. These future historians and anthropologists would likely conclude that most of us simply had little concern about environmental pollution and, at best, engaged in conservation activities that occasionally amounted to more than virtue signaling. The second group, composed of philosophers, would ignore archaeological testimony about the activities of the population, the geologic evidence of our environmental impact, and other documentary information, focusing instead on our philosophy—the writings of those of us who made explicit philosophical arguments in journals and university press books. There, they would find a lively discussion about the nature of harm wrought by environmental degradation and its paramount significance for humankind, suggesting that contemporary humans cared a great deal about pollution and valued their environment very highly indeed. Both groups of scholars, of course, would be right, given the scope of their disciplinary concerns. But their portraits of our beliefs could not stand at a greater distance from each other.

Something similar applies in the case of Nahua philosophy. Philosophers aim to articulate the logical connections among various statements and to assess their validity. They do not try in the least to represent the thoughts of the common people. In ancient Greece, for example, Plato and Aristotle advanced views which would have been thought thoroughly bizarre by most Athenians. Plato, in the Republic, infamously has Socrates argue that ideal family arrangements should allow for incidental incest.[13] Aristotle, for example, held that "god" was the first principle of physical motion.[14] But the unpopularity of such views makes them no less worth studying, for the philosopher. Likewise, these discourses would have expressed the views of an elite minority among the Nahuas and would probably stand at odds with the views of many commoners.

Such focus on nonrepresentative views has implications for terminology. Philosophers infamously contort language into a technical vocabulary suitable for their needs. In Homer's *Odyssey*, Odysseus finally gains permission to leave Calypso and build a raft to venture home. In the Greek text one reads that Odysseus goes to gather *hylēn*, a form of the noun *hylē*, meaning, "stuff" or "materials."[15] In Aristotle's metaphysical philosophy, however, *hylē* takes on the technical meaning of "prime matter." One of the principal wagers of my translation is that something similar may be identified in the philosophical discourses of the Nahuas; my philosophical glossary at the end of the volume aims to illuminate the specifics more directly.

Thus, the philosophical view which follows engages only indirectly with most anthropological and historical treatments of these matters. Just as philosophers do not treat the Greek understanding of pollution, *miasma*, as a significant topic, so the present account does not treat the historical discussion of *tlazolli*, filth, as a significant topic. It is not the burden of historians and anthropologists to do philosophy, so my omission should not be taken as a slight against the scholarly quality and importance of their work.

Louise Burkhart's study of Nahua ethics is the most widely esteemed historical treatment of the topic in the English language, and justly so. Burkhart presents her study as an analysis of metaphorical tropes "which relate elements from separate semantic domains."[16] Specifically, the study follows the way in which certain terms in the early colonial period, such as *tlatlacolli* (error), become something else in the adaptations of Christian clergymen, such as a metaphor for "sin." Her chapters carefully trace the literal and conceptual translation of these tropes. Among the significant historical implications of her study is that the simple "replacement" theory of indigenous culture by a European one is mistaken, even in moral contexts.

Philosophical ethics begins with the aim of answering a different set of questions; not necessarily those that matter most to historians, but those that matter to the discipline of philosophy. These include the following four clusters. First, did the Nahuas have a conception of the good life—a life that people should be aiming for as opposed to whatever they do aim for? Second, did they have criteria for discerning right action? If so, what were they? Third, how did they think of these topics as related to our psychological abilities to act on what we should do? Finally, in what source did their views find a logical home? Did they, for example, think of right actions as the result of God's decree? Or did they instead think of their source in whatever could be reasonably discerned by reflecting on human life and its circumstances? These questions, briefly, range over the four main areas of ethics as a discipline in philosophy, which concerns: the good, the right, moral psychology, and metaethics.

My study of the philosophical outlook of the Nahua is thus often consistent with Burkhart, but it approaches matters differently. Burkhart observes, for example, that the Nahuas had no sense of "good" and "evil" as one finds them in Christianity. Instead, they focused on "terms expressing disorder and decay." Below, I focus on the Nahua's concern with ordering and arranging, which is a positive expression of the same notion. Likewise, Burkhart argues that the Nahuas do not have an abstract sense of what would be absolutely good, even when they use *cualli* and *yectli*. I agree, and yet my translation focuses instead on a sense of the good life that the Nahuas did articulate, along with something approximating what "Western" philosophy calls virtue.

There is more to be written about the metaphilosophical dimension undergirding a translation of this sort, not only for interdisciplinary purposes, but also because the Nahuas deserve the "honorific" status of being classed among the "philosophical" peoples of history. I hope these points prove sufficient for now, so that we might turn to the contents of that philosophy itself—as best as I understand it.

Nahua Metaphysics

In his essay "On What There Is," W. V. O. Quine writes: "A curious thing about the ontological problem is its simplicity. It can be put in three Anglo-Saxon monosyllables: 'What is there?' It can be answered, moreover, in a word—'Everything'—and everyone will accept this answer as true."[17] Nearly the opposite could be written for Nahua metaphysics.

Nahuatl has, properly, no words at all, much less three words, that could express the basic problem of ontology. Moreover, the Nahuas have no term for "to be" and no grammatical equivalent to the English copular "is."[18] While they do have a metaphysical outlook, the fact of the matter is that our English word "ontology" derives from the Greek participle ōn, "being," so in a strictly etymological sense, the Nahuas have no "ontology."

Rather than having words, Nahuatl has wordal sentences called "nuclear clauses."[19] What are called "nouns" in the language are nouns only by analogy with Indo-European nouns, since they tend to be translated that way in those languages. Strictly considered, one may write *michin*, or "fish," with the meaning that "it is a fish." It is unsurprising, given these points, that the language has no singular copular term and can get by in sentences without it, even in an implied sense.

Linguistics experts have classed Nahuatl not only as an omnipredicative language but as a paradigmatically omnipredicative language.[20] A first, though inaccurate, way to think about this is to say that everything is a verb in Nahuatl. What there is, flows. More accurately, "omnipredicativity" is a paradigm concept. It holds that to be classed as an omnipredicative language, that language must lack a copular term—e.g., "is" in English—and have a certain number of ten other properties that individually contribute to the omnipredicative strength of the language (the more of them, the stronger). One example of these additional properties is that the language uses a zero-morph to indicate the third-person singular of verbs—meaning that "he," "she," and "it" are not marked by any specific "letter" (morph) when conjugating the word. The points are technical, but the take-home idea is that Nahuatl exhibits all such characteristics and so is maximally omnipredicative. This matters philosophically because, while it is true that languages do not constrain thought totally, it is also true that they do make certain modes of approaching the world feel more natural.

For the Nahuas, the world is best and most easily conceived as a process of evolving relationships. In their own terms, the Nahuas conceive of the basic energy of the universe as *teotl*.[21] All things are made of *teotl*, and yet *teotl* does not exist beyond our world. I am made up of *teotl*; you are made up of *teotl*; even our excrement is made up of *teotl*. Yet this basic energy is also held to be divine—not a personal god, like the Christian Jesus Christ, but "divine" in the sense of worthy of our respect and awe. Also, it is thought to be something sacred. Because *teotl* is everything and everything is in *teotl*, the universe, our natural world, is divine. For these reasons the Nahuas are classed as pantheists, which is the view that holds that all (*pan* in Greek) is god (*theos* in Greek).

But the discussion so far moves too quickly. To be clear, this area of study is new and there is not yet any settled consensus among scholars.[22] In my own view, *teotl* is rather too abstract to be taken as the basic sense of reality for the Nahuas. In a way, there is no basic building block from which other things are built up. While the mind is able to distinguish different features of reality, such as *teotl*, each dimension appears to be incomplete and spills over into the next.

Our reality, in fact, is a series of relations, usually doubles, called *inamichuan* (singular: *inamic*). Some of these doubles take familiar forms, such as male and female, hot and cold, night and day, here and there, left and right, and so on. The Nahuas also had some unfamiliar pairs, such as the numerals 9 and 13. As I understand the matter, *teotl* is an abstraction of sorts, since what there is turns out to be *teotl* as some coordination of these basic relations. In other language, *teotl* expresses itself in doubles, so that He~She is always *ometeotl*, because *ome* means "two." Mostly literally, *ometeotl* means the "Dual Divine."

This view has some direct support in existing texts. Yet, even if it proves slender and contestable, it is also consistent with some of the more common names for *ometeotl*, and so enjoys an explanatory adequacy that rival views do not enjoy. For example, one name is *Tlo-que Nahuaque*, which means the "Lord of the Near and the Nigh." To explain, you can think of it this way: since God is everything, then God is omnipresent, and so always near, always nigh. Yet, this god is also called *Ipalnemohuani*, often translated as "Life Giver." More literally, it is the One by Whom We Live. That name indicates a true property, for if God is nature, by what else could we live? Finally, this god is described as *Yohualli, Ehecatl*, the Night and Wind. This might be plausibly thought to designate an omnipresent god, because one can hardly see at night, cannot notice the wind directly. Understood in this way, *ometeotl* is that god that we know hardly at all, and only indirectly.

Ometeotl, as the fundamental energy of the cosmos, thus expresses as doubles. These doubles, moreover, are related to each other in an holistic way—all are connected to each other. The whole that expresses that relationship is called, in the Nahuas' metaphorical language, a "sun." Following the tale that has come to be known as the *Legend of the Suns*, they held that there were four such previous formations, and that the humans who existed in them were of a different character, so that they even had different foods for sustenance.[23] We presently live in the fifth sun, called *nahui olin*, or four-movement. The kind of movement at work, however, is a specific form of undulating and wavelike movement, which is why legends held that our sun would collapse in a great earthquake. For the Nahuas what there is, what exists at present, is thus *ometeotl* as four-*olin*. But *ometeotl* appears to designate all possible suns. In that sense, *ometeotl* expresses most closely what we call "being," while the fifth sun most closely approximates what we might call "existence."

The possibility of the sun's collapse sets a basic existential and broadly ethical task for Nahua peoples: Fight! Fight to keep this sun alive! The task is broadly ethical since, even though the Nahuas held that our sun would collapse, they also thought there was meaning to be had and something beautiful to be won in this struggle against the forces of entropy that we cannot defeat. The character of this struggle did sometimes entail warfare, which involved the notorious public executions that the Spaniards exaggerated and called "sacrifices."[24] But the far more central goal was to order and arrange.

Ordering and Arranging

In a recorded speech, part of the discourses of the elders sequence that is recorded in volume 6 of the *Florentine Codex*, our largest surviving selection of the Nahua's worldview, a newly installed king speaks to the people of his city and articulates the ideal person, both for men and for women. The image is nearly the same one, so I will quote the one that speaks of the man, which makes the point at issue most succinctly. The king describes him this way:

> And he is revered, in truth he is known as a sustainer. He becomes the great ceiba, the Montezuma cypress, next to and by which people take refuge.[25]

There are two separate trees discussed in this passage, the silk cottonwood and the Montezuma cypress, also called the ahuehuete (Spanish; in Nahuatl the term is *ahuehuetl*). If you have ever witnessed these majestic trees, you will have noticed not only their size, but also their great root structure, which keeps them firmly placed on the earth. They form, unsurprisingly, part of the Nahua's metaphorical constellation of terms and images that express the good life.

I have called this general ideal the rooted life, since metaphors for it include strong trees, standing on one's feet, and living the truth.[26] The

Ceiba trees in Guatemala (left) and in Palm Beach, Florida (right).

last of these metaphorical terms, *neltiliztli*, is literally "verification-ness," but it may be connected etymologically to the term for "root" (*nelhua-yotl*). If that were right, then the true life and the rooted life are linked etymologically and the whole constellation makes sense. Nonetheless, it seems unlikely to me that definitive linguistic evidence will emerge on this last point, so I think it more accurate to hold that "rootedness" is an apt term in English to designate the metaphorical constellation of notions at work in Nahua philosophy that cover the good life. The problem is a cultural one. The Nahuas, especially for their important terms, often refused to make use of just one word or phrase. They preferred many for the reasons I articulate below on Nahua aesthetics. So, I am

An ahuehuete in Santa Maria de Tule in Oaxaca, Mexico.

using "rootedness" here to cover the whole constellation of metaphors as a kind of shorthand—something not very Nahua, but that *we* have come to expect in the "West."

The way that one performs this rooted life is to live with excellence or virtue. In Nahuatl there is a phrase that expresses this notion, *in cualli, in yectli*.[27] Such excellent action is performed at the personal level by ordering and arranging the principal features of one's character. The Nahuas used another expression to discuss character in this way: they called it one's face and heart, *ixtli, yollotl*. Those were thought to be the seat of one's judgment and the seat of one's desires, respectively.[28] With respect to one's personal character then, the virtues just are the excellent arranging and ordering of one's face and heart.[29]

Yet the Nahuas are unique in their approach to the virtues. Just as they conceive of reality as a process of relationships, so also do they understand human agency primarily by way of shared agency. Our virtues, they think, are enacted *with* others in the ideal case—especially for deliberative purposes. Practical wisdom, in short, is a feature of wise groups and not only of individual agents. One of the primary ways that these wise groups enacted this practical wisdom was through rituals.

Rituals are for us rather arcane practices. I was raised Catholic and had twelve years of Catholic education. Even after all my time studying the Nahuas, my immediate sense of a ritual concerns practices such as standing, sitting, kneeling, and taking communion. For the Nahuas,[30] rituals were far broader and often much looser in scope. They concerned everything from the observance of calendrical feasts to the daily routines of youths in school. We don't tend to think of morning routines as a ritual, but with only slight modification the Nahuas might have. Above all, rituals allowed the Nahuas to coordinate their activities together in an ordered and arranged way.

As an example, consider the exercise of practical wisdom when merchants deliberated before departure to foreign cities. The description that follows is from the *Florentine Codex*, which devotes an entire volume to the merchant class. The ritual observed began by consulting with a day reader (a soothsayer), who would undertake an activity to determine which day was most propitious for departure. The night before departure, a ritual sacrifice—of small animals, most likely—would be performed to secure good fortune. Finally, on the morning of the departure date, the leader of the merchant group hosted the leaders of the local neighborhoods, the *calpoltin* (singular: *calpolli*), to deliberate about the practical conditions of travel. He welcomed them, and they replied in kind. The text reads as follows:

> And when he [the host] had thus spoken to them, then the principal merchants of all the neighborhoods, the leaders of each *calpolli*... responded to his words. When in the case that the host had means and invited guests, then they sat in order by rank. At one side, by the wall on the right, were the principal merchants; and on the other side, starting on the left, sat the other sorts of merchants, the sort that spies in enemy territories. Capping the ends were the youths.[31]

You will notice immediately that our term for "merchant" does not precisely track the Nahua notion. We class "spies" as a different sort of group than "merchants," but for the Nahuas, they were people who also traveled to foreign capitals for specific reasons and faced dangers in doing so.

What matters for philosophical purposes is that the process of group deliberation is thus structured to differentiate the participants both by background, as the spies are separated from the trading merchants, and rank, which in this case follows both from experience and nobility.

Often the elderly occupied positions of higher rank, having accrued relevant experience in life's course. The youths, though not excluded from the discussions, were positioned in the place of least importance, on the ends. In the deliberations that followed, the topics ranged from known difficulties in travel conditions to admonitions to respect the customs of other people and how to behave in foreign lands.[32] The passage thus suggests that while all might participate in the group deliberation, not all opinions were equally weighted. There is a reason some sat at the center, having developed more of the qualities conducive to excellent deliberation, and some at the ends.[33] The purpose of the organization was thus to recommend action for each traveler's good life, both practically and with respect to broader interpersonal conduct, making it an explicitly ethical discussion.

The entire process developed a sensibility about practical wisdom that is quite unlike typical forms found in the "West." Aristotle, perhaps the prototypical expositor of "Western" virtue ethics, conceives of what he calls the *phronimos* as an ideally wise *individual*. His reasoning seems to have been that in the ideal case a wise person wouldn't have to ask someone else for advice. The Nahuas, by contrast, think that in the ideal case, one finds the advice one needs in a good group.

This difference in approach entails that Nahuas also conceive of the relationship between person and polity rather more closely than one finds in "Western" thought. Recorded among the discourses of the elders in the *Florentine Codex* one finds a speech wherein an elder priest installs a newly appointed king. The priest calls out to *ometeotl* as the Old God, the mother and father of gods, as follows:

> And may [the new king] not blemish, besmirch the reed mat and
> seat—your reed mat and seat, your glory, your honor, your rule. . . .

O master, o our lord, may he arrange, may he order for you
upon the reed mat, the reed seat, the place of honor.[34]

Just as we are to govern ourselves, ordering and arranging our face
and heart, the king is to order and arrange the city—which is expressed
through a double metaphor in Nahuatl: *atl* and *tepetl*, water and mount.
The king is to order and arrange for the city while on the throne, also
called by a double name: the reed mat and the seat. In doing this he takes
on the role of the dual god, *ometeotl*, thus effecting the cosmic process
that maintains the fifth sun. These activities of ordering and arranging
pairs, unsurprisingly, extend beyond personal ethics and political activity to aesthetic considerations.

Nahua Aesthetics

Aesthetics, in the "West," is a domain of philosophy typically concerned
with questions about how the fine arts represent something and for what
end. For example, the eighteenth-century German philosopher Immanuel Kant taught that they represent what is beautiful, at least after a
fashion.[35] Most scholarship on Nahua aesthetics has traveled this path
too, searching for the representative qualities of their art and architec-
ture, their songs, poems, and dances.[36] But relatively recent advances in
our historical understanding of their practices of fine speech (*tecpillatolli*) have suggested that the question of representation was, for them, at
least of secondary importance.

James Lockhart, in a series of investigations, has shown that the
structure of arrangement at work in Nahua fine speech enacts a broader
metaphysical principle that might be called the cellular principle of orga-

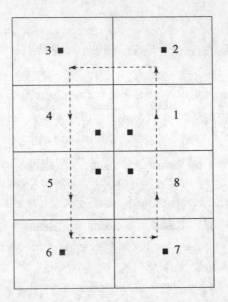

An idealized image of an Aztec *altepetl* (city) with eight *calpoltin*
(neighborhoods) represented as rectangles. The black squares represent
the locations of the primary buildings in each *calpolli*. The dotted lines
represent the direction of rotation for obligations, and the numbers
represent the order of rank for each *calpolli*. (Replicated from James
Lockhart [1992], p. 37.)

nization.[37] To understand what is at stake, it will be easier to begin with
large-scale physical structures rather than high prose and poetry. We
might start with the Nahua "city."

A Nahua *altepetl* is often called a "city," but the organization of the
political entity is rather different than the English term indicates. It
included not only the central buildings such as the temple and market, but also the surrounding land and obligations related to its culti-
vation for the residents. Moreover, it was not conceived as a basic unit,
but was built up from *calpoltin*. That term literally means "large houses,"

but has a sense more closely approximating a neighborhood and semi-independent ethnic group.[38] Each *calpolli* had its own "god" and thought of itself as unified, even if not all members were biologically related. Moreover, each *calpolli* was divided further into smaller districts that might be called wards, which then divided into individual households.

It is likely that each *calpolli* began as an individual unit, but as soon as it grew large enough, it would subdivide into separate units, just as cells divide after they grow. When those new units grew too large, they would separate again. And while there is evidence that some ethnic groups preferred seven units, mirroring the myth of the original seven caves from which humans were thought to emerge, most divided into units of four, six, or eight. Their organizational growth thus followed the broad pattern of Mesoamerican doubling. This also suggests that they conceived of organization by way of symmetry in the way that cells grow in a plant or flower.

These *calpoltin* would take turns contributing goods to the city (*alte-petl*) in a rotational scheme, which was rank ordered. The leading *calpolli* would be the leader of the united city, which functioned to direct the scheme of contribution. The image on page xxvi is a reproduction of one found in Lockhart's research. It illustrates an idealized and simplified city (*altepetl*) composed of eight *calpoltin*. The four central *calpoltin*—numbers 1, 4, 5, and 8—have their temples and central buildings positioned in close proximity; these are represented by the black squares. The outer four *calpoltin* have their central buildings distributed at a distance from the others. When Europeans arrived in Mesoamerica, they looked for what they thought were cities after the European style. As a result, they often identified the central conglomerations of buildings as a "city," and ignored the rest. Yet, the Nahuas would have included both the buildings and the surrounding land as part of the *altepetl*. Moreover, it is the direction of obligation, as represented by the arrows, that orders and arranges the *calpoltin* into an *altepetl*.

The cities that are best known historically, including Tlaxcala, Chalco, and Tenochtitlán, were not so simple as the previous paragraph suggests. These real cities (*altepetl*) were composed of structures like the idealized form above but included their own unique rotational schemes for contribution. Moreover, their central rotational schemes organized other cities (other *altepetl*), which themselves organized *calpoltin*, which organized wards, which organized households, in which each person found their own social role, which facilitated the organization of each person's face and heart.[39] The illustration on page xxx, which is my own adaptation of Lockhart's schemas, shows a few of the differences.

The Nahua *Tlahtoani* was a person whose office is typically translated as "king," but the term also means "speaker" because they spoke for the people of their *calpolli*. What distinguished the king from the leaders of other *calpoltin* is that he would have directed the highest-ranking *calpolli* in the rotational scheme—taking spot 1 in the diagrams above. Such kings included Motecuhzoma in Tenochtitlán and Nezahualcoyotl in Tetzcoco.

Eventually, even these complex cities (complex *altepetl*), such as Tenochtitlán and Tetzcoco, grew and merged into one another by way of alliances. What is often called the "Aztec Empire" was in fact nothing but a merged, strategic alliance among three complex *altepetl* at the time of the Spaniards' arrival. It consisted of Tenochtitlán, Tetzcoco, and Tlacopan.

The process of cellular division and organization, then, might have continued indefinitely. Each "cell," or *calpolli*, divided when it grew too large but maintained an organized relationship with its other "cells," through a symmetry of obligations to cultivate and use the land under protection. Such growth by symmetry was, roughly, the cosmic sense of excellence and beauty. In a line, if matters developed well, then the cosmos could be likened to a flower. Unsurprisingly, one finds that Nahua art, and especially fine speech, enact the same pattern.

All fine speech (*tecpillatolli*, which literally means "noble speech") uses the same principle of growing symmetry. To understand how it works, we might start with a metaphorical trope called a *difrasismo*, which expresses one idea metaphorically by way of two key terms. Here are some further common cases.

Nahuatl Phrase	Literal Components	Paraphrased Meaning
in tocolhuan in tachtonhuan	our grandfathers and great-grandfathers	ancestors
in quiahuac in ithualco	the exit, the patio	household
in mitl in chimalli	the arrow, the shield	war
in petlatl in icpalli	the mat, the seat	authority
in cozcatl in quetzalli	the jewel, the quetzal feather	one's child

We saw a few of these above, including *in cualli, in yectli* for virtue. One might now appreciate their broader significance in Aztec aesthetics. Such statements are most commonly found in the *huehuetlatolli* texts, where the frequent use of *difrasismos* beautifies the prose by way of ordering and arranging.

Like the cellular organization of cities, these metaphors pile up in an artfully crafted *huehuetlatolli*, balancing each other and extending the beauty of the phrase.[40] In the present work, one might look at paragraph 60 as an example of what is at stake. It begins as follows:

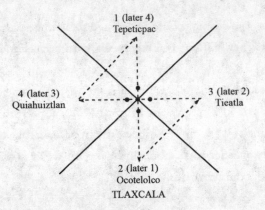

1 (later 4)
Tepeticpac

4 (later 3)
Quiahuiztlan

3 (later 2)
Tieatla

2 (later 1)
Ocotelolco

TLAXCALA

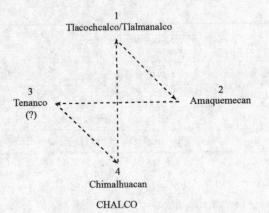

1
Tlacochcalco/Tlalmanalco

3
Tenanco
(?)

2
Amaquemecan

4
Chimalhuacan

CHALCO

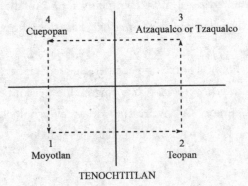

4
Cuepopan

3
Atzaqualco or Tzaqualco

1
Moyotlan

2
Teopan

TENOCHTITLAN

My necklace, my quetzal plume, as precious metal is forged, as jade
is pierced, so you have been forged, so you have been pierced. With
necklaces, quetzal plumes I am endowed. One lip, two lips I here
wish to bind on your ears.

The metaphors in this statement are piled up and balanced, like a complex *altepetl*, with the result that an outsider has almost no chance of
making sense of them without assistance. The present translation thus
includes copious footnotes to guide the reader. The role that they play,
however, is like that of building beauty from organized doubles. Nahua
fine speech is not metered and versed, but rather balanced and bloomed,
which is to say symmetrically composed by organizing *difrasismos* into
larger complex units. Moreover, each speech, if it is complete, is balanced by a response from the younger person, using metaphorical language that is similar to what the elder employs. The final principle of
symmetry at work, then, is enacted between the elder and the younger
person through the respect they show each other mutually. Like the
city, the symmetry of a discourse turns on the balance of obligations
among the participants.

The principle is continued, most elaborately, in Nahua poetic song,
which goes by the name *xochicuicatl*, or flower songs.[41] Like the *altepetl*,
there is a cellular unit at work in the *xochicuicatl*. Instead of the *calpolli*,
it is the verse. Each verse is divided into a semantically meaningful sec-

Opposite: James Lockhart's reconstructed image of three Aztec complex
altepetl: (a) Tlaxcala, (b) Chalco, and (c) Tenochtitlán. Each of these complex *altepetl* is made up of smaller *altepetl*, which are numbered to signify
their rank. The top-ranking *altepetl* for Tlaxcala, for example, is Tepeticpac. The dotted lines represent the direction of rotation for obligations.
(Adapted from James Lockhart [1992], p. 22.)

tion and a section of vocables—literally meaningless utterances—that would have been sung. The semantically meaningful section also has two parts, one which is wholly complete in the verse, and another (at least in the classical case) that is shared with the verse pair. Exactly how much is shared among verse pairs varies and indicates the strength of connection between the verses. What follows is an example of a strong pair (the "*y ahua yya*" portions are the vocables that cannot be translated).

> Do nothing but enjoy, each one enjoy, my friends. *Will you not enjoy, will you not be content, my friends? Where will I get fine flowers, fine songs? y ahua yya o ahua yia yiaa ohuaya ohuaya*
> One never spends two springs here. I am afflicted, I Quaquauhtzin. *Will you not enjoy, will you not be content, my friends? Where will I get fine flowers, fine songs? y ahua yya o ahua yia yiaa ohuaya ohuaya.*[42]

As each verse remains self-contained, so too does each verse pair. Their meaning, then, retains the basic cellular autonomy, but replicates it at a higher order through symmetry.

As one might expect, the process continues its "growth." Just as the city (*altepetl*) forms an organizational unit of neighborhoods (*calpoltin*), so a flower song (*xochicuicatl*) forms an organizational unit of verse pairs. A whole song, then, is almost always composed of an even number of verses. Ideally, they form a unit of eight, though in larger cycles, the poetical analog of complex *altepetl*, six- and ten-versed pairs are common. What follows is an eight-verse flower song, as Lockhart translates it.

1. The flower-plumed quechol bird enjoys, *enjoys above the flowers. An ohuaya.*

2. Sipping the various flowers he enjoys, *enjoys above the flowers. An ohuaya.*

3. Covered with green leaves are your body and your heart, Chichimec lord Telitl; your heart is jade, it is flowers of cacao and fragrant white blooms. *Ahua yyao ayya yye. Let us enjoy! A ohuaya.*

4. You come intertwined with smiling flowers on the flower tree, on a mat of flowers from paradise; the flowers swell, rootless flowers. From within flower plumes you sing Tlailotlac; you are fragrant, you are intertwined. *Ahua yyao ayya yye. Let us enjoy! A ohuaya.*

5. We are not twice on earth, noble Chichimecs; let us enjoy. Flowers can't be taken to the land of the dead, we only borrow them. *In truth, we must go. Ohuaya.*

6. Ah, in truth, we are going, we are leaving the flowers and the songs and the earth. *In truth, we must go. Ohuaya.*

7. Where do we go? Where do we go when we die, do we still live? Is it a place of enjoyment? Does the Giver of Life still wish entertainment? Perhaps only here *on earth are* there *sweet flowers and songs. Enjoy, each one, our wealth and our garments (of flowers). Ohuaya.*

8. Enjoy, noble Chichimecs, for we must go to the home of Popocatzin, Tlailotlac Acolhuatzin. You will (?); no one will remain. *On earth are sweet flowers and songs; enjoy, each one, our wealth and our garments (of flowers). Ohuaya.*[43]

There is one point of difference in cellular organization between the city (*altepetl*) structure and the flower song (*xochicuicatl*) structure. In the flower song, a unifying whole is achieved through a satisfying symmetrical scheme, while in the city that same unity is achieved through a fixed order of rotation. Both approaches, however, enact the same basic model of beauty as symmetrical growth.

The task to order and arrange, then, courses through every dimension of Nahua life—from our interior spaces, in the balancing of our face and heart, through to the arrangement of social roles, cities, elevated prose, and poetical song. It also explains how Nahua ethics culminates in a series of basic insights about the relationships among beauty, our human vulnerability, and our cosmic fragility.

Beauty, Fragility, and the Good

The cosmos, composed of matching relations (*inamichuan*) that are then ordered and arranged into a "sun," persists precariously. This precarity translates into our personal lives. The path to a good life, which in this translation is what the father aims to teach his son and the mother, her daughter, begins with a basic insight. The Nahuas put it in a memorable expression: "Slippery, slick is the earth."[44] This means, in part, that we will "slip up" in our lives, but also that others will fail us too. The Nahuas reason that all our actions are subject to an impressive degree of luck, so that whether those actions go well or poorly is often beyond our individual control. Finally, the Nahuas think that even our cosmos is fragile and that our age will pass just as all the others have. As a result, the Nahuas think the good life to consist of learning to take a stand on the slippery earth.

Of course, the Nahuas agree that we would all like a life free from pain and filled with pleasure; we would all like "happiness" in the colloquial sense of that term in English. But they reason that pain and pleasure are something like *inamic* pairs, like hot and cold or day and night. In one discourse, a father addresses his daughter as follows, making this point clear:

O my daughter, my child, hear well: the earth [*tlalticpac*] is not a
good place. It is not a place of happiness [*pacoaia*] or satisfaction.
"It can only be said that the earth is a place of joy-fatigue, joy-pain,"
so the elders often say. That we may not go weeping forever, we are
in debt to Our Lord, Who gave us laugher and sleep, our food and
strength, our life and love.[45]

There is no simple experience of happiness, in short. Rather, we experience cycles of joy and fatigue, or joy then pain. They follow on each other
like two sides of a coin, so that aiming for happiness in this sense is no
more reasonable a project than aspiring to grow seven feet tall.

Besides, the Nahuas would insist, you don't really want a happy life
anyway. You just think that you do. To make that intuition clear, it may
be easier to reflect on a "Western" example—on the choice that Odysseus makes in book 5 of the *Odyssey*.[46] Although it takes Odysseus ten
years to return to his homeland after the battle at Troy, he spends much
of that time on an island paradise with the goddess Calypso. While ini-
tially pleased, after a time Odysseus laments his fate, and the gods take
pity on him. Hermes informs Calypso that she must let Odysseus go,
and she agrees, provided that she might have one last attempt at con-
vincing him. In the next scene they sit across a table and she offers him
what any mortal would apparently want: agelessness, immortality, and a
romantic, leisured existence on the island with her. Odysseus turns her
down, and in the next scene he leaves to chop wood to make a raft and
sail home in search of his wife and child.

At first, this is a puzzling story—the opposite of the biblical Genesis,
where Adam and Eve are forced to leave Paradise. Odysseus chooses to
leave. But then again, how many of us would choose to have all those
goods if the price paid is that we could never see our loved ones again *and*
that they would never know what happened to us. This is the father's

broader point to his daughter in the speech quoted. It is also the father's point to his son in the present translation (see especially paragraphs 8 through 11). What you want is a meaningful and worthwhile life, and if you need to make sacrifices for it, then so much the worse for happiness.[47]

The difficulty that remains is this: Even if we are aiming after rootedness rather than happiness, how do we achieve it? Especially, what are we to do about the fact that we tend to slip up, that others slip up in trying to help us, and that much of our fate is out of anyone's control?

One of the strategies that the Nahuas use is to rely on others to facilitate our ability to live well. We are to be like the Montezuma cypress and ceiba for others, eventually, but as we grow and develop, we live largely in the shade and protection that others provide. The earth is slippery after all, so our best shot is to work to stand on our feet with the help of other people—our lovers, friends, family, community, society, and in the widest respect, nature (*ometeotl*) itself.

Performing that rooted existence well means leading a virtuous life, and although the Nahuas do not appear to have elaborated a theory with central virtues, one can find in their writings a repeated emphasis on five such virtues, all of which are conceptually linked.[48] Principal among the virtues, discussed above, is practical wisdom. This has the role of discerning the mean (*tlacoqualli* and *tlanepantla*) for right action, so that it is involved in the performance of all the virtues.[49] Some of the crucial virtues that support its operation are humility (*tololiztli*),[50] temperance (*mimatiliztli*), bravery (*in quauhyotl, in oceloytol*), and justice, which, in its broadest sense, is the path (*in ohtli*).[51] All of these virtues parallel to some degree what are called the "cardinal virtues" in the "West." Yet humility, or literally the bowing of the head (*tololiztli*), is unique. The reason for its presence in this list, however, is not difficult to discover. In order to deliberate well in a group, you must be willing to accept the reasons of those who are more expert than you are on a topic, and that requires humility. For the Nahuas, this humility extends to following traditional customs in most circumstances, since they embody time-tested wisdom.

A problem yet remains. Suppose we agree that learning to stand on the earth, to grow roots, to follow the path, requires that you and I learn to act virtuously. Even if this is our best chance to live well, the Nahuas still think that the configuration of our sun is bound to collapse. What, then, is the point of any of it?

The Nahuas thus have a different strategy of response to this broader problem. Unlike the Christian cosmos, in which the salvation of our lives and justification of our finite existence is to be found in an infinite and eternal afterlife, the Nahuas have no similar notions. One of the three animating forces of our bodies, the *yolia*, lives on after us[52] in the afterlife for four years in a journey in the Land of the Dead (*Mictlan*). It is helped by a little yellow dog and by family on the earth who make what people today call *ofrendas* (Spanish: offerings). But at the end of that journey, that energy merges with the impersonal energy of the cosmos, with *ometeotl*, and that's the end of our individual personality.

These points bring us to the primary way in which the Nahuas understand a virtuous life. Rather than justify our existence through an eternal afterlife, the Nahuas seem to hold that the immutability of our existence, the fact that it is in a certain way, will be enough, if we live it well. It is important to understand that the excellent living of our lives, their performance, just *is* virtue. The good life isn't a product, like the pot that a potter makes, but a performance, like a dancer's dance. In more philosophical terms, the good life is intrinsic to your actions, not extrinsic to them; virtue constitutes them, it is not the cause of some other consequence.[53] You can't maximize this sort of life apart from living it well, with more virtue.

When that kind of life is lived, when it orders and arranges well, when it is "straight or right" (*yectli*) and "good or wholesome" (*qualli*), it has the

worth of a dance well done on the world's stage. And just as an impro-
visational piece does not lose its value if it is not recorded, neither do our
lives lose value for not being eternal. Just as a poem is not more beautiful
for being longer, so are lives are not more valuable for lasting a century.
Our lives, our relationships, our earth, then, are all fragile and evanes-
cent arrangements. None of that counts against their worth, at least not
if they are good ones. It is in this sense, in the beauty of a struggle against
entropic forces that we cannot win, that Nahuas hold that what is beautiful and what is good coincide.

These points articulate the outlines of Nahua metaphysical, ethical,
and aesthetic views. All dimensions are evident in the present discourses
to varying degrees. Some topics are significantly deepened. It was with
a mind to bring these features forward that I undertook to translate the
present work. Yet, the current text, like most that have survived from
the contact era, has a complex history. Chief among these complexifying
factors stand the dual layers of Christian interpolation that run through
it. To clear the way to an articulation of what sensibilities guided the
philosophical translation of this work, it proves helpful to have in mind a
sense of its historical character.

A Brief History of These Discourses

Doctor Alonso de Zorita, *oidor* of the Royal Audience of Mexico in
1544, described these discourses in glowing terms as follows:[54]

> Beyond raising their children with the discipline or care which
> has been discussed, the [indigenous] fathers themselves sustained
> their children by giving many and very good counsels, and they,

the principal Indians, have those discourses even today in memory by way of their paintings, and a quite old religious man in that land [i.e., Mexico] ... and they retrieved them from their paintings, which are like writing, and they understand quite well from them, and [the recording friar] did not change a letter from what they told him, beyond dividing the discourses into paragraphs ... and that the names which they gave their gods [the friar] advised that they discard those and put instead the name of the true God and Our Lord.[55]

One notices immediately that a prominent member of the Spanish Royal Audience thought well of these discourses, and he was not alone in this estimation. In general, it appears that humanists of the era thought well of them and that even the religious authorities of the Catholic Church thought likewise, as they ultimately proved responsible for their publication.

At the same time, one cannot help but note that the original friar who recorded these notes made substantive changes by deleting all the names of the gods and replacing them with Christian names or titles. Though the discourses appear to have been recorded in Tenochtitlán, Tetzcoco, Tepeyacac, Tlaxcala, and Tepepulco, the differences in the gods to whom the original Nahuas would have appealed have thus been effaced. Some measure of the richness of these names, and their metaphysical implications, are thus lost.

Nevertheless, these discourses also look to have been passed down through the generations in the screen-folded "painted books" called *amoxtli*. It is by looking at these and reading them, Zorita tells us, that the principal indigenous "religious man" retrieved these discourses. In studying the matter Ángel María Garibay K. concluded that these discourses may have stretched back to the thirteenth century of the common era, and though he wrote that assessment some seventy years ago, there is still no overriding reason to doubt the antiquity of that provenance.[56]

The man who first recorded these texts was the Catholic father Andrés de Olmos. He was charged with the task by the Royal Audience of Mexico, and supported in this charge by local prominent clergy, in 1533 CE "because he had the best command of the Mexican language [i.e., Nahuatl] at that time in the land."[57] His charge, as the sixteenth-century chronicler Gerónimo de Mendieta relates, was double. It was to record in order to better refute what was in need of refuting and to save what ought to be saved. The mold Olmos followed, then, was that which Christians had followed in reappropriating pagan thought from Greek and Roman philosophers.

Olmos also made use of these recorded discourses for his *Arte de la lengua mexicana*, one of the earliest grammars of Nahuatl, which was completed in 1547. In that work he includes the longest of the present texts' discourses to provide an example of the many metaphors used by the elders in their eloquent speech. Since that text does not include later additions and alterations, it may yet permit a more authentic version of the present work. Nevertheless, that sample is quite short, and, insofar as the present text is a completed artifact that can give present scholars a window onto the syncretic thought of early colonial Mexico, it is worth treating in its own right.

Yet there is a second stage of elaboration and augmentation for the present text, which owes its existence to another friar of the same convent. Juan Baptista Viseo, who was also a Franciscan, some decades later found and collected the discourses from which Olmos had transcribed among the recorded documents in the Convent of Santiago Tlatelolco. After interpolating a few points and adding a series of speeches at the end of the work to make them suitable for the purposes of converting and guiding the indigenous youths of his era, Baptista Viseo was supported by local authorities in publishing the completed work in 1600. Baptista Viseo originally titled this work as follows (translated from Spanish into English):

> *Huehuehtlahtolli, which contains the talks that fathers and mothers made to their sons and daughters, and lords to their subjects, all filled with moral and political teachings*

It is this work, which has been preserved and reproduced in facsimile form, that the late Librado Silva Galeana transcribed and rendered in 1991 into a most literal Spanish translation. The present translation is based on Silva Galeana's transcription of this work, with any deviations from his interpretation of the original facsimile footnoted where necessary.

The resulting historical artifact presents a puzzle for scholars that is not typical for philosophical works—namely, to discern what in the text is of indigenous origin and what is syncretic in character. At points, undoubtedly, the task of separating one from the other may be likened to peeling a raspberry. More often, however, the task resolves into a matter no more difficult than peeling bananas. For example, in the first discourse, starting at paragraph 3 and continuing through paragraph 6, the presence of Christian terms and metaphors dominates. It is not difficult to discern, as a result, that these are not original to the discourse. To anyone who is working in the original Nahuatl, the clumsiness with which the typical metaphors are handled, or the simplicity of the grammar employed, also becomes an obvious cue. The final portions of the work, from paragraph 142 to the end at 202, are indisputably a Christian interpolation written with the purpose of training future priests and medical doctors from among the sample of younger native boys in the area.

A translator of this text is thus left an uncommon set of questions that turn on how to treat obvious interpolations. Since these problems are new for philosophical translators, I shall here note three of these typical problems I encountered and the solutions I used, for better and for worse, in treating them.

The first sort of common problem concerned terms that shift in meaning from their use in indigenous contexts to Christian contexts. In Homeric Greek, the term *hamartia* means an "error." In the New Testament, it means "sin." A similar set of contextual shifts is present throughout this work. For example, the Nahuatl *tlatlacolli* means a "harm" or "wrong." Just as the early Catholic clergymen did with *hamartia*, so their later colonial counterparts pressed *tlatlacolli* into meaning "sin." In response to this problem, when I thought the context sufficiently Christian, I have rendered it "sin." Otherwise, I have most commonly rendered it "harm." The same sorts of considerations guide terms such as *ihuiyan*, "peacefully"; *icemele*, "gently"; and *yocoxca*, "calmly." In more Christian contexts such terms might come to mean "tranquility," "joy," or "peace," but in a philosophical context I must take steps to disambiguate what is at work from conceptions of the good life as the ancient skeptics held (e.g., with *ataraxia*).

A second set of considerations turns on demonic and unchristian figures. The most prominent among these is the *tlacatecolotl*, or "owlman." In indigenous contexts, this figure is associated with the ability to make use of occult and mysterious forces—often for nefarious ends, though perhaps not exclusively so. The early colonial fathers, however, settled on this term as a best approximation for a devil or the Devil himself. I have translated the term literally in almost all cases because the strangeness of the use would have been similar for an indigenous Nahua. To

make the character more intelligible, I have also included my own philosophically informed translation of the description of these characters,
from volume 10 of the *Florentine Codex*, in part II. Similar considerations,
then, hold for the *ahuianime*, the "pleasure women," and like figures.

Finally, there is the matter of treating hybrid and Spanish terms as
they appear in the Nahuatl texts. By hybrid terms I have in mind cases
such as *"padreme,"* which uses the Spanish base *padre*, "father," with the
pluralizing ending *"me(h)"* from Nahuatl. By Spanish terms I have in
mind cases where an unaltered Spanish term such as *Dios*, or "God,"
appears in the original. In cases such as these I have generally tried to
leave the original untranslated. The reason is that *Dios* would have stood
out as much to a native Nahuatl speaker is it does to an English speaker.
When that strategy proved unworkable, I footnoted the differences at
work. And with that, the discussion has already slipped into philosophical waters. Let's turn to the topic squarely now.

A Philosophical Translation

A philosophical translation is unlike other translation efforts, since it
is guided by disciplinary sensibilities about what is important to the
discipline in its current state. In the present case, it is the status of
ethics, in its many branches, that guides the sensibilities at work. In
following this course, I have tried to split the difference between two
competing needs.

The first need might be termed a concern for isomorphic precision. It
is this need that guided Allan Bloom in his translation of *Plato's Republic*
into English.[58] He was concerned that the Greekless student would not
be able to understand Plato well given existing translations. As a result,
he sought to provide a text with terms so rigidly faithful to the origi-

nal that one might learn Plato in English as well as Thomas of Aquinas learned Aristotle in Latin. The grammatical differences between English and Greek, however, are far greater than those between Greek and Latin. As a result, by Bloom's own admission, the gap proved too great for the sort of precision to which he aspired. Yet the aim, to render one term in English for one term in Greek, remains an aspiration for any philosophical translator.

Since there are even fewer specialists of Nahuatl than there are of ancient Greek, this purpose weighed more heavily for me. Nahuatl stands even further from English than English does from ancient Greek, so that isomorphic precision proved proportionally more elusive. Still, I have endeavored to render the core set of philosophical terms—where those contexts are not obviously Christian—consistently. I have also aimed to render the philosophical meaning of *difrasismos* apparent whenever those appear. To facilitate the reader in understanding some of the choices made, I have provided a philosophical glossary at the end and copious footnotes throughout.

Some examples might better demonstrate what I have in mind. Consider a common *difrasismo* with weighty ethical importance: *in qualli, in yectli*, which literally means "good, right," but plays the role that philosophers understand by the terms "virtue" and "excellence." In the first discourse, a father speaks to his son as follows:

> *Ye qualli, ye yectli, xicmocuitlahui in tlalticpacayotl; xitlaay, xitlatequipano, xiquaquahui, xelimiqui, xinopaltoca, ximetoca; yc tiquiz, ye, ticquaz, ye ticmoquentiz, ye yc tihcaz, ye yc tinemiz. (par. 25)*

Silva Galeana's quite literal Spanish translation, when rendered into English, reads:

> It is good, it is correct that you take care of worldly things; labor,
> work, pick up firewood, work the earth, plant nopals, plant
> magueys; from that you will drink, eat, dress; from that you will
> stand on your feet, with that you will live.

Silva Galeana's aim is to render as literal a translation as possible in Spanish and he succeeds admirably in this aim. Yet, because his purpose was
not philosophical, the text lacks the precision our discipline needs. The
difrasismo "*yectli qualli*," which appears in the construction "*ye qualli, ye
yectli*" in the original, is not given an ethical rendering. Instead, Galeana
treats it as an emphatic phrase, so that it means, in effect, it is *very good*
that you do the following things. As a result, the passage also fails to connect the proposed activities with the way of life under discussion.

A philosophically informed translation, the one I have devised, reads:

> It is enough for virtue that you take care of worldly things. Work,
> labor, gather wood, till the ground, sow cactuses, plant magueys. It
> is from that which you will drink, eat, dress. With that it is enough
> for you to stand, for you to live.

This translation makes clear that the activities at stake are ones tied to
a social role, constitute a form of excellence, or virtue, and connect to
a way of life. Moreover, the *ye* construction in this statement, literally
meaning "already," looks to play a logical role—namely, to indicate sufficiency. Both the ethical and logical dimensions are thus evident in the
present volume.

Since so much of *The Discourse of the Elders* is ethical in character, cor-
rections like these are to be found on nearly every page. They prove, then,
too numerous to list here. To give you a sense of the more common cor-

rections present in this translation that follow from philosophical interests, here are seven of them.

1. In Nahuatl, the future tense often caries a normative sense. Rather than use the future indicative "will," it will be clearer to the English reader if the modal "should" is used. For example, in paragraph 18 in the father's instruction to his son about conduct while traveling, one reads: "And so that you will not be taken for a knave, when you go on the road, you should look not at one place and then another. You should only strive ahead on the march. You should not go clapping your hands, nor zigzagging on the road. You should not go being carried on the shoulders of others, nor lean on them." By rendering each instance of the future tense with "should," the ethical obligation at work is clarified.

2. The term *nehuiyan*, for example in paragraph 10, does not mean "will." Our term, used to translate the Latin *voluntas*, is an important notion in "Western" ethics that seems to have developed sometime later than Aristotle's discussion of *prohairēsis* in the *Nicomachean Ethics*. To avoid implicating *nehuiyan* in this "Western" discussion, I have rendered its appearances using the phrase "by one's own accord" or similar circumlocutions.

3. Terms for prudence carry special philosophical significance, since they define what is intended by practical wisdom. I have reserved "prudence" for forms of *imati* made suitably general or appearances of *ixtlamatiliztli*. In paragraph 16, for example, the appearance of "*ticnehmachiliz*" does not mean to make your word prudent, but to be judicious in responding. At stake is not a general sense of practical wisdom as philosophers understand it.

4. In this vein, it proves crucial to distinguish *imati*, which means "deftness" or "knowledge informed by experience," from forms

of *tlamati*, which concern what in the "West" is called theoretical wisdom.[59] The latter is also the source of the name for philosophers in Nahuatl: *tlamatinime*.

5. The social role of warriors, designated by the *difrasismo* "eagles and ocelots," often serves metonymically for courage, a virtue. In paragraph 27, for example, the father justifies his actions to his son saying he has acted in this way "because the character of the eagle and ocelot (*in quauhyotl, in oceloyotl*) has matured, has grown well in me." The virtue, and not primarily the social role, is at stake here.

6. Similar points apply to the topic of vice. A "perversion" is a Christian notion while "vice" is an ethical one from the indigenous view. When, in paragraph 17 *tetlahuelilocatili* appears, this means not that the actions under discussion "pervert people," but that those actions "make people vicious."

7. Finally, it remains important to distinguish causal sayings from specific virtues. Among the Nahuas, humility is a virtue. The appearance of *ycnotlacayotl* (in paragraph 34) does not raise the discussion of humility as a virtue but serves rather as hyperbole for frugality.

The second need that animates the present translation turns on a point that Jay Garfield raises in his translation from the Sanskrit of Nāgārjuna's *The Fundamental Wisdom of the Middle Way*. He worries that in rendering too literal a translation one risks turning what is familiar in the original into something bizarre in the translated text.[60] It is, of course, this concern that has animated Stephen Mitchell's many translations, and it animates Michael Bazzett's poetic translation of the Mayan *Popul Vuh*.[61] In the Spanish translation of these discourses, over-literalization is a deliberate feature of Silva Galeana's work, since his aim was to facilitate future translations of these discourses. In that respect, his work is nearly an interlinear textual study along the lines of Allen J. Christenson's translation of the *Popul Vuh*.[62] But that approach leaves a significant gap for the philosopher, since it is integral to the Nahua ethical view that the aesthetic dimension be taken seriously. This is, after all, one way in which the Nahuas arranged and ordered.

In an earlier draft of this translation, I hoped to follow the course of Albert Cook and Frank Copley, who rendered the hexameter of Homer's *Odyssey* and Lucretius's *On the Nature of Things*, respectively, into iambic pentameter in English with beauty and precision.[63] The difficulty that I encountered in rendering these discourses into iambs was not that it proved an impossible task, but that it accomplished the wrong end. Nahua noble speech (*tecpillatolli*) achieves its aesthetic aim not through meter or verse, but through balancing metaphorical units. One thus remains more faithful to this non-"Western" aesthetic if one uses the natural proclivities of English for elision and concision to achieve that balance in metaphorical construction.

To spell out in more concrete form how the present translation achieves this end, I note the following items. First, it proved necessary to change the order of some *difrasismos*. Paragraph 8, for example, uses the phrase "stone and stick" as a metaphor for negative consequences. This is more naturally rendered into English as "stick and stone." Similar considerations apply to the Nahuatl "hair and head," which in English read more naturally as "head and hair." Beyond idiomatic alterations like these, I introduced a small number of grammatical changes that I shall again list with the aim of facilitating comprehension—and of circumventing frustration by my fellow *nahuatleros*.[64]

1. Often Nahuatl uses the determiner *in* in a series, where in English it is more natural to use the conjunction "and" or have no article at all. I thus rendered these with "and" or with no conjunction.

2. Long, mounting phrases will, in Nahuatl, repeat possessors and verbs, but this proves unwieldly in English, which prefers progressive elision. I thus elided.

3. At times those phrases will also link terms by juxtaposition where English prefers conjunctions. *Difrasismos* such as "*in tinocozqui, in tinoquetzal*," meaning literally "you my necklace, you my quetzal plume," read with improved ease when rendered with a conjunction as "my necklace *and* quetzal plume."

4. Various grammatical clauses which imply results or purposes only weakly prove difficult to render as such in English. The pervasiveness of *ic* in this text, with its multifunctional grammatical uses in Nahuatl, for example, requires decisions that cut down on the range of meanings in Nahuatl. I have simply supplied the narrower interpretation in English that I thought best.

5. Diminutives in Nahuatl and Spanish (e.g., in par. 23) have no living analog in contemporary English, and so are translated variously as reverential, diminutive, and "dear." Spanish has clear advantages as a modern language on this score.

6. Some terms lack definite or indirect objects in Nahuatl but need one to read well in English. For example, "*otlacauh in moyollotzin*" is literally "you have granted your heart," but in English it makes far more sense if rendered as "you have granted your heart *to me*."

7. Finally, the Christian interpolations that pervade the work like the marbling in a slab of meat are often awkward in the Nahuatl. To be faithful to this characteristic—one that diminishes the aesthetic qualities of the original—I have rendered these interpolations in a similarly clunky way. Thus my translation oscillates between beautiful poetic metaphor and rough, rigid prose. This is mostly how the piece feels in Nahuatl.

One consequence of following the path outlined is that some of the paragraphs in these discourses border on the unintelligible to the uninitiated: the entry into the Nahuas' philosophical world may feel like a plunge into some deep waters. I urge you to take it anyway. The results merit the efforts. The translation could not avoid, as a result, many running footnotes. More such footnotes are provided at the beginning of the work to help you along, while in later paragraphs I have assumed that you are now familiar with the terms. Also, it's worth noting a final point on orthography. The Nahuatl language of the early post-colonial period, from which these texts derive, had no standard way of transcribing the oral language into written Latin letters—the ones using the Latin alphabet, which you're reading right now. I have endeavored in this work to spell terms in a generally acceptable way, but in some cases, I have used the spelling available in the text itself. Scholars will not be disturbed by the variance since it is quite common. Yet, beginners will be enabled to poke around in the original texts and find the matching words. That's how I started my own path and I'd like to encourage others to do likewise. Now, to prepare for your first jump, I leave you with something of a philosophical compass.

A Philosophical Compass

The first and major part of this book is devoted to the *Discourses of the Elders* as Olmos first recorded them and Baptista Viseo later revised them. They contain roughly four central topics. The first topics, which run from paragraphs 1 through 56, address how to live. Unlike the familiar formation of the question in "Western" philosophy, the Nahuas would have asked not "How shall I live?" but rather "How shall we live?" The exhortations the father and mother make to their son and daughter, respectively, urge a life following the path (*in ohtli*), rather than the way of the deer and rabbit, i.e., the bestial life.

The second set of topics (par. 57–94) concerns stages on life's path. While still set in opposition to the life of the deer and rabbit, the principal concerns here turn on familiar inflection points in one's life. In a parallel set of discourses in the *Florentine Codex*, volume 6, you will read both descriptions of the role of the "baptism" as a Nahua ritual and a series of detailed admonitions for women. In this translation, such baptism discussions are not present, and the discourses that cover the stages of life for women seem either to have been dropped or not recorded in the first place. Rather, this volume's discourses primarily follow the son as he grows from infant status to adolescence, to the age at which he may marry, to the toils of adulthood, and finally—if the age of the elder giving advice is any guide—into the later years.

The discussions then move onto the topic of justice as it receives its more specific formulation through Nahua institutions as the rule of law in paragraphs 95–122 and 135–41. These paragraphs also distinguish the different obligations that nobles were thought to have that separate them from the discourses with commoners of the earlier paragraphs. Rather than strictly older figures admonishing the young, in these paragraphs, nobles admonish one another. In doing so they articulate what an ideal ruler and nobleman ought to do.

Finally, the cycle of discourses ends with Christian interpolations in paragraphs 123–34 and 141–202. What was likely to be an explanation of the social role obligations that follow for a medical doctor or midwife (*ticitl*) is here changed to become a discussion about the obligation a medical doctor has to bring those who are sick over to the Christian faith, so that their souls might not perish and be punished in the afterlife. Beyond that description, the final paragraphs are lessons crafted for those who would join the priesthood. It is tempting to see in these nothing but Christian thought, but matters are never so simple. The need to press Christian notions into Nahuatl results in a syncretic Christianity, and the topic proves essential to understand how later seventeenth-century philosophers, such as Sor Juana Inés de la Cruz, may have developed their thought from this context.

The second part of the book contains a series of descriptions of social roles among the Nahuas as recorded primarily in volume 10 of the *Florentine Codex* by Sahagún and his team of indigenous informants. I have selected these so that you might better understand the people discussed in these discourses. They center primarily on knowledge workers, and the descriptions show that the Nahuas clearly distinguished between philosophers, priests, and those who worked with occult forces. Also included are descriptions of controversial figures, namely the owlmen and pleasure women. Any attempt to translate these passages often turns on an holistic sense of one's understanding of the topic under discussion. I can only underscore that, especially with respect to these translations, the intellectual work is thoroughly interpretive. To balance my view, I have supplied copious footnotes, and I hope the present introduction grounds the place from which I translate.

The field of Nahua philosophy remains an incipient enterprise. I stumbled onto it only when, as a graduate student, I found a copy of Miguel León-Portilla's *La filosofía náhuatl* in my university library while looking for a different book. Immediately, I was absorbed in the topic, and perhaps to the consternation of my advisor, it derailed my studies for a week. But it mattered to me personally, because I am of Mexican heritage and my maternal grandmother used to confuse our family by mixing up her Spanish with Nahuatl. It also mattered to me professionally, since I was unaware that philosophical texts of Nahua philosophy even existed. The willful silence surrounding its existence constitutes a clear epistemic injustice, and so I thought it self-evident that we would do better philosophy if we were to take it seriously.

After endeavoring to study the language and field for some years, I worked up the courage to write León-Portilla about some points that turned on his view of *ometeotl* and he replied quickly and graciously. I'm not sure that we ever came to full agreement before he passed in 2019. My friend James Maffie has an excellent book on Nahua philosophy, yet we too disagree significantly on some key points in metaphysics and ethics. Another friend in the field, Alexus McLeod, has a vastly different view than I have on personal identity among Mesoamericans. David Bowles, a fellow *nahuatlero*, and I have discussed points of translation and I do think we found some points of common ground, but on others we might still stand at some distance. This is the present state of Mesoamerican philosophy. It is young and I find such disagreements both exciting and productive. The life of the mind requires us each to do our best and to state our honest views, so that we can make whatever advance in knowledge proves possible. The present translation, the first of its kind, is but a first, wobbly step forward in this domain. I hope, at least, that it provokes you to think and reflect about the goals of human life. That was, after all, the original purpose of these discourses among the Nahuas themselves. If it succeeds in this aim, then, to some degree, a silenced philosophy will have found a hearing, and what was once killed will in a certain way have returned to life. And there would be something fundamentally Nahua in resurrecting what was destroyed, just as humans were said to have been revived after four previous deaths in the *Legend of the Suns*.

Notes

1. An indication of this point is the success with which Peter Adamson's podcast "History of Philosophy without Gaps" has met, the wide readership that Bryan van Norden's popular pieces, developed philosophically in his (2017) work, has received, and my own essays written for public audiences, which have "gone viral" on *Aeon* and related popular outlets.

2. "Western" philosophers had been, of course, interested in the "Orient," and Confucianism in particular, since the seventeenth century. Both Gottfried Leibniz and Christian Wolff read Confucius's works with fascination and care. It was Immanuel Kant who first began the European movement against the consideration of other philosophical traditions. For more on this point see van Norden (2017), 19–29. Since Kant's time, it has been ignored and derided in the anglophone world, with a small number of exceptions. With respect to indigenous philosophy, some early attempts in the twentieth century looked promising, as one finds with Radin's (1927) study, which was endorsed by John Dewey. But that interest looks to have waned by, or perhaps because of, the Second World War. With respect to the Aztecs, specifically, while early German anthropologists found affinities with "Western" philosophers, the first serious treatment of their work as philosophy is to be found in León-Portilla's (1956) study. That book, titled *La filosofía náhuatl*, was almost entirely ignored by philosophers until the twenty-first century. The title that it still bears in English translation, so unready was the anglophone world to believe that Aztec philosophy existed, is *Aztec Thought and Culture*. It was not until James Maffie's (2014) that a title granting the Aztecs philosophical status existed in the anglophone world.

3. Latin American philosophers, including Walter Mignolo (2005) dispute this term. The concern, simply, is that the "West" is a self-designation, while the peoples of this culture designated others with their own terms. The name itself, in short, introduces a colonial frame.

4. It was this limitation that led Alfred North Whitehead to undertake what he called speculative philosophy in (1978), 3–13.

5. For more on this point, see Purcell (2018).

6. See Alfredo López Austin (1980), vol. 1.

7. For a detailed exposition of Aztec embodied psychology, see ibid., vol. 1, chs. 5–7.

8. See Purcell (2017).

9. The canonical formulation of right action for a virtue ethics that I have in mind is Rosalind Hursthouse's (1999).

10. For Aristotle's account of the *phronimos* as an individual, see his *Nicomachean Ethics* VI.5, 1140a24.

11. For example, the *Bancroft Dialogues* might be better titled *Bancroft Discourses*. These were collected around 1570–1580 in Tetzcoco, which was the great city just on the opposite side of the lake from Tenochtitlán. It records the speeches of Nahua nobles and was intended to teach ecclesiastics the niceties of polite conversation in Nahuatl. There is a philosophical discussion to be had concerning the relationship between Platonic "dialogues" and these Nahua "discourses." I have decided to leave some conceptual ground for this discussion and have followed the more dominant translational tradition in using "discourses." Perhaps, however, they are philosophically the same.

12. The term *nahuatlacah* does appear in colonial-era texts and it does refer to the people themselves. It is, however, comparatively rare.

13. The point is at least implied as a logical possibility in Socrates's second "ridiculous" wave in Plato (2003), V.457d–473b.

14. The entire purpose of Aristotle's (1957) book lambda is to argue for this point.

15. Homer (1917), V.257.

16. Burkhart (1989), p. 13.

17. Quine (1980), p. 1.

18. This is a strong claim, but I base it on strong linguistic evidence. For those interested in the linguistics discussion, see the opening eight chapters of Andrews (2003) and see Launey (2004).

19. I am adopting this terminology from J. Richard Andrews (2003).

20. See Michel Launey (2004).

21. See James Maffie (2014).

22. I agree with much of Maffie's view. Yet, his view stands in opposition to Miguel León-Portilla (1956), who takes *ometeotl* to be basic. My position, some of which I articulate in Purcell (2018), develops both views. As Alexus McLeod (2018) argues for the Maya, I have come to conclude that for the Nahuas the search for basic entities is a mistake, or at least misleading, since each dimension is incomplete. What there is, is the all, and while the all is in motion, I think the more relevant feature is that it lacks full determination. If one were to continue asking after further dimensions of specification, e.g., not color, not red, not scarlet, but the exact hue of a material, the Nahuas would deny that such exists. What there is, after a point, is fuzzy. It is only this approach, I think, that makes sense of the way in which Nahuatl lacks the perfect aspect, at least as we, native Indo-European language speakers, think of it.

23. See the *Codex Chimalpopoca*, 2.7–43.

24. The topic of blood sacrifice is, of course, one of the most well-known features of Nahua culture. Like almost everything else about this people, it is not well treated in public discourse. Matthew Restall (2018, ch. 3) presents considerable

evidence to reconceive the typical view as an artifact of Spanish self-legitimating writings and suggests that most such activities, where persons were killed, more closely resembled what we in the "West" would call public executions.

25. *Florentine Codex*, vol. 6, ch. 14, p. 67.

26. See especially Purcell (2021) for my treatment of the etymological connection among terms.

27. *Florentine Codex*, vol. 6, ch. 7, p. 31; cf. "vice" as *acualli, ayectl*" at ibid., p. 32.

28. Ibid., vol. 6, ch. 9, p. 44.

29. Note that in the same speech, the ruler laments being unable to govern himself, making the parallel between governing others and one's own person explicit (ibid.).

30. And I mean the pre-invasion Nahuas, not the 2.5 million ethnic Nahuas alive today.

31. *Florentine Codex*, vol. 9, ch. 3, pp. 12–13.

32. One should note that the text is elliptical. It records that "all [of the *calpolli* leaders] responded to his [the principal merchant's] words" (ibid., vol. 9, ch. 3, p. 12), but the recorded text retains only the discourse of the leader positioned in the leading position. He warns generally of weather conditions but details moral conduct in cities abroad.

33. The children, including even those who are not able to carry heavy materials, are set to go traveling to gain experience. They will have a mirror, a *tezcatl*, held up for them (ibid.).

34. Ibid., vol. 6, ch. 14, p. 19.

35. Plato's discussion of artistic representation in book X of the *Republic* (1968) stands at the heart of the question of representation for the "West." I have in mind also Kant's *Critique of Judgement* (1987).

36. For example, see León-Portilla (1956) and Octavio Paz (2014), pp. 404–52.

37. This is Lockhart's claim in (1992), p. 15.

38. Lockhart notes that in fact *tlaxilacalli* is the more common term used for a fixed territory and that *calpolli* was used more for the migratory phase of the Nahuas (ibid., p. 16).

39. And each "face and heart," technically, is a metaphor for the organization of the three primary animating entities on one's body; these resided in three primary areas but were distributed into thirteen embodied areas, each of which contributed to thinking and acting. Such forces, moreover, were infused through various cosmic means, such as the sun's rays or the food one ate.

40. Miguel León-Portilla, in what is part of a larger study, has compiled likely the most exhaustive list of aesthetic characteristics for Nahua *tlahtolli* (discourses) (2018), pp. 296–308. The present section is indebted to his insights.

41. This portion is again all Lockhart's research and I quote his translations at length because they are, likely, the most neutral ones available on central questions that are presently highly contested among scholars. They do tend to obscure the metaphysical dimensions that might interest philosophers, but they prove more suitable here to identify the aesthetic principles at work.

42. *Cantares Mexicanos* (Bierhorst, 1985), p. 218.

43. Ibid., pp. 346–49.

44. *Florentine Codex*, vol. 6, ch. 41, p. 228.

45. Ibid., vol. 6, ch. 18, p. 93.

46. Homer (1917), 5.77–147.

47. Clearly, this sense of happiness tracks our colloquial use in English, which generally reflects the experience of elevated emotional states. At stake is not a deeper sense of happiness, either of the Aristotelian sort or even of the all-things-considered sense of happiness that contemporary utilitarians, such as Roger Crisp (2008), advocate.

48. Dan Russell (2009) has a worked-out sense of cardinal virtues and the Nahuas had no similarly articulate scheme. It would take one beyond the evidence, then, to argue that there were five cardinal virtues in Nahua ethics that held some sort of systematically articulated relationship. What I propose is merely a reorganization of their scattered statements. The terms selected in what follows are probably the clearest terms to indicate the ideas at work, but it is helpful to recall that the Nahuas used many terms. It is our penchant to search for a single word, not theirs.

49. For evidence, see *Florentine Codex*, vol. 6, ch. 9, pp. 100–101; ibid., vol. 6, ch. 22, p. 125; paragraph 34 on *imati* in the present translation. This is known as the reciprocity of virtues thesis, and so differs from the unity of virtues thesis. The latter holds that all virtues are one. The reciprocity of virtues thesis is weaker, holding only that all virtues are related. The Aztecs hold to this thesis because they distinguish the modes of operation for a virtue. These include virtues centered on "emotions," "dispositions," enacted by one's social role, and those enacted in a social rite. Socrates can hold to the unity of virtues thesis because he subscribes to the view that if one really understands what is right, one will act on it—a view called Socratic intellectualism. Plato and Aristotle disagree, because they both think that reason can be overwhelmed by appetitive desires (*epithumia*) and the desire for honor or recognition (*thumos*).

50. See the father's admonition to his son: ibid., vol. 6, ch. 12, pp. 106, 110.

51. For specific determinations of justice, read the discourses of judges to the people in Sahagún 1997, fol. 61v, col. A–63r col. B.

52. At least, this was the fate for those who die natural deaths. I am setting aside discussions of those who die as warriors, during childbirth, and other special

cases, which are sufficiently complex to deserve their own separate treatment. The general existential problem about the value and meaning of human existence can be addressed without averting to this set of considerations.

53. Consequentialists, whether utilitarian or otherwise, are teleological in their ethical orientation, but differ rather significantly on this point. The matter, then, distinguishes their view from the virtue ethical position on the character of virtues in relation to the good life. This is the point that brings the Aztecs into closer proximity with Plato and Aristotle. For a detailed explanation of this point, see Purcell (2017).

54. This section is deeply informed by Miguel León-Portilla's study of the text, which he presents as the "Introductory Study" for the most current Spanish translation of the text that Andrés de Olmos compiled (1991). It is also helped by Josefina García Quintana's two essays on the *huehuetlatolli* (1974, 1976) as was León-Portilla's exposition.

55. The translation is my own from Zorita's statement in his *breve y sumaria relación*, 112–13, which I have taken from León-Portilla's longer quotation (2011), pp. 15–16.

56. Ángel Maria Garibay K. (1953–54), p. 444.

57. Gerónimo de Mendieta (1945), vol. 2, bk. 2, prologue.

58. Plato (1968).

59. Technically, the abstract substantives for prudential wisdom and theoretical wisdom in Nahuatl would be *neihmatiliztli* and *tlamatiliztli*, respectively.

60. Garfield in Nāgārjuna (1995), p. ix.

61. *The Popul Vuh* (2018).

62. *Popul Vuh* (2007).

63. See Homer (1967) and Lucretius (1977).

64. This is a hybrid term between Nahuatl and Spanish, used by many of us who are Chicanos. It means "a person who uses or speaks the Nahuatl language."

Part I

THE DISCOURSES OF THE ELDERS

Exhortation in which the father speaks and edifies his son as follows so that he may live virtuously

1. My son, my necklace, my quetzal plume,[1] you have life, you have been born. You have come to earth,[2] to the land of our Lord. You were forged, you were shaped, you were born by the One by Whom We Live, *Dios*.[3] Before you and above you,[4] we, your mothers, your fathers, have observed. So too, before you and above you, have your aunts, your uncles, and your relatives observed. For you too have they wept, for you too have they suffered as you came, as you were born on the earth.

2. And now, for a short time, you have come to look, you have come to grow, you have come to sprout your stalks. You have come to fatten up, as if you were a little bird barely able to peck. You have grown as if you had just come out of your little shell, as if you had wrapped yourself in precious wares, as if you had sprouted your little tail and wings. As you move your little hand, your little foot, your little head, so you move as if you were already trying to fly.

3. And perhaps for a day, perhaps for two days, however long the One by Whom We Live determines, shall we borrow you as our own, shall we borrow a necklace, a quetzal plume. Thanks to our Lord,

---

1 This phrase is a *difrasismo* for a child.

2 The term "earth" here and later is *tlalticpac*.

3 In the Nahuatl text, the Spanish term *Dios* is used.

4 This is a phrase that literally means "in front of you and on top of you," and in some contexts means that a person is acting disrespectfully, out of their station, or leaching the labor of others. In the present context, however, such dependence is thought to be appropriate, so the arrangement is respectful.

perhaps you will stand, perhaps you will live on earth. May you exist, may you develop in peace, in joy.

Place yourself beside the Lord, our Lord, not with haste, not without consideration, so that He may have mercy on you.[5] And may He know it, may He still test you, may He appreciate your worth, for He is God, a leader, very much a protector, a person who carries you on his back, and He is quite powerful. Because He, *Dios*, is your very mother, your father, He takes great pains to take good care of you, to love you much more than I love you, I who am your mother, your father.

4. Because He said it, thought it, determined it,[6] for this you have lived, for this you have been born. Forget Him not in the day nor in the night. Go invoking Him, go praying to Him, go sighing, go grieving. Do not sleep, do not rest in tranquility. Do not let your face, your heart fail before Him, our Lord, because He is your father, because He formed you.

Through His generosity, serve Him lovingly so that you might be helped, so that His heart may grant, so that He may give you His gifts, that which you are worthy of, your merit, your standing, your maintenance. With that you will be able to stand, with that you will be able to live and not wander into the clouds, into the darkness.

5. And wherever you pass in front of the image of our Lord, or of His beloved ones, or of the Cross, you will honor them very much; you will bow down before Him or bend the knee. And it is much better

---

5 This passage and the next, paragraph 5, look to be an interpolation. Beyond the Christian language and metaphors, the reasoning for right action changes here. The purpose clause "*inic mitzmotlaocoliliz* / so that He may have mercy on you" uses external reasons to motivate right action. These reasons are not obviously consistent with the discussion of living excellently on *tlalticpac* that follows in sections 7–13.

6 This paragraph recalls John 1:1, "In the beginning was the word."

if you go out in front of the very body of our Lord Jesus Christ (who is within the Holy Sacrament). In that way you will beseech Him with all your heart because He is your God, because He is your Lord, because He is your Redeemer, because He is your venerated Father who is within the Holy Sacrament. And you will honor the name of our Lord Jesus Christ very much, and on His feast day you will adorn yourself quite well.

6. And you will welcome His children wherever they are or wherever you find them: those of lineage, the rulers and those who preside over the people, those who guide in divine matters, those who rule, the Fathers,[7] and also the old man, the old woman, and the needy, the wretched, the unhappy, the joyless. For that reason they are to be greeted, and you, therefore, should greet them, not just carelessly, but with quite good words. You should not live as if you were mute. If you conduct yourself well, then so will you be known, so will you be revered, and so will you be praised.

7. And love, thank, respect, fear, be afraid, obey, do what the heart of the mother, of the father, wants, because it is their due, because it is what they merit, because it is their gift, because service, obedience, and respect may be counted among their possessions. For he cannot stand, he cannot live who does not obey, who does not want to serve them, who does not want to honor his mother, his father, who lives in front of and on top of them.[8] For he who does so shall be called an ingrate. In

---

7 In the original Nahuatl, the hybridism *padreme* appears. Recall that a Catholic priest, or "father," is a *padre* in Spanish.

8 In essence, "who lacks respect for them." The verb *nemi* here means not only "to live," but "to make one's way" or "to follow a path." This is the person who makes one's way by putting themselves first. It approximates what philosophers today call an ethical egoist. In the next sentence the person is named an *ycnopillahueliloc*, which means an "ingrate," but its etymological components also suggest an "evil

short, do not lead a disorderly life; do not run about thoughtlessly; do not go about imprudently in the presence of, next to, the people. Live only peacefully, only gently, because it is sufficient for virtue.[9] Humble yourself, bow with respect, lower your head, bend your neck.

8. And speak well to people, petition them, respect them, fear them, obey them, and love them, because that is how you will live, that is how you will stand. Do not follow the principle, the path of the one who is over there, who leads a life in that place, who goes around drunk, who makes his way getting drunk, who spits in his hands, who makes fire with his hands, who keeps something on his neck, who keeps something in his hand, who ties his pants tightly, who hits his hip, who hangs from above, who shouts, who yells, who screams as if he has consumed mind-altering herbs, mushrooms, or as if he had drunk pulque. He no longer thinks about the stick and stone,[10] but receives them quickly. He feigns concern for and raises his shoulders to his mother, his father. He no longer respects them, he only turns against them, he turns around, he no longer fears them, he no longer considers them in anything, he only yells and shouts without reflection. He no longer goes out by the exit, no longer lives in a place for living, no longer runs in a place for running.[11] There he no longer has eyes, there he no longer has ears, there his face and heart are not well. He no longer sings the song, no longer speaks the

---

orphan." This is the same phrase used in paragraph 1 and rendered "before you and above you" there, because the context was respectful.

9 This is the *difrasismo* "*cualli, yectli*," used with the particle "*ye*," which is typically translated as "already." A more literal translation would read: "because it is already good, because it is already right."

10 These are consequences that are negative and, in legal contexts, punishments.

11 These are metaphorical ways of expressing the idea that he does improper things.

word. No longer in his moment of shouting does he shout, but instead he speaks.[12]

9. He no longer follows the principles, the path. He no longer listens well to the good word, that which elevates, that which explains. Only without reflection does he walk. He flees constantly, he falls suddenly. He lives only disheveled, lives only in excrement. No longer with tranquility, no longer with joy does he rise, does he go to bed, for thus he hastens like a rabbit, he hastens like a deer. He goes about intoxicating his brain, he goes about confused. And from there he does not leave, he does not want to be carried away, he does not want to be reformed. He slips out of people's helping hands, slips away. He kicks, he repels them with his foot. He can no longer be held, he can no longer be caught, he can no longer be subdued. He only pushes, throws himself at people. He only hits and strikes people. He only growls at people unexpectedly, only bites them suddenly.

10. And this one, who has gone contrary to the Lord's great desire, will no longer extend his hand where he should have extended it, will no longer go to settle where he should have settled, will no longer go to enter where he should have entered, nor go to die where he should have died. Because only a snare will he go to hunt, only a rope will he go to put on.[13] Because only to the ravine, because only to the cliff he will go to look. And into them he will go.[14] Because only with the stick, only with the stone will he be struck. Because only in the grass, only in the forest he will settle. There he will become food for the vultures, for

---

12 Meaning that his words become indistinguishable from mere utterances, noise vocalizations.

13 This is a metaphorical way to express that he will suffer.

14 In the Nahuatl, he will literally meet or join or be paired with them.

the coyotes. For only against the stone fences and on the walls will he go to throw himself. And so will he become food for the dogs, because he made himself a rabbit, he made himself a deer. Because by his own accord he made himself, he habituated[15] himself into vice,[16] into wickedness. Because by his own accord he became intoxicated, drunk, just as if he put on hooves, became feral, became a rabbit, a deer. He found the plain, the path of the rabbit and the deer. By his own accord he went into the forest, into the grass. By his own accord he approached the corners, the walls; he was ruined, he went astray. By his own accord did he throw himself into the river, did he go overboard. And no longer will anyone be bothered by him, for him.

11. And do not laugh, do not mock, do not make fun of the old man, the old woman, the one who is sick, the one with a crooked mouth, the blind, the one-eyed, the one-armed, the one whose hand is hurt, the one whose hand is cut off, the cripple who walks on all fours, the lame, the one who drags his foot, who drags his hand, the mute, the deaf, the insane, the demented.[17] Do not mock he who is diseased, or he who suffers wrongs, or he who did, who committed wrongs in front of you.

12. All these things I say to you. In no way should you laugh at them, should you mock them, make fun of them, make jests of them, shame them, abhor them, detest them, loathe them, despise

---

15 The verb for "habituation" here is the reflexive mo-piqui, to "form oneself." In other texts one finds uses of piya, to "guard" or "watch," in extended phrases, such as "to guard in the chambers of one's heart."

16 The difrasismo for virtue in the negative: ahqualli, ahyectli—the not wholesome, not right.

17 In Nahuatl, these terms for people with disabilities have the reverential and diminutive suffix -tzin.

them. Only thus will you arrange, only thus will you be on guard, only thus will you be afraid, only thus will you fear, only thus will you weep, only thus will you grieve, only thus will you humble yourself, only thus will you bow down before our Lord, so that it may not happen to you as it would happen to you if you had laughed at them, if you had joked at their expense, if you had despised them.

13. And so, is it best[18] that you go near to, that you come up against what makes people sick, what torments them, what frightens them, what scandalizes them, what depresses them? For how long will you come to feel envy, will you come to be frightened? When will you come to say: "It is certain, they, my mother, my father, said only the truth, they told me so. I should have listened; I should have accepted what they said. I should not have mocked those people, I should not have made fun of the creatures of God; I should have loved them, I should have pleaded with them, I should have helped them, I should have seen them with joy, I should have consoled them so that what is happening to me now would not happen. For now, I have come to meet, I have come to approach what makes people sick, what torments them, what afflicts them: their hunting snare, their rope, their hook, their nettle, their stick, and their stone—those of our Lord. They have already drawn near to me, already come next to me. He has taken me, He has seized me, where shall I enter, where shall I go?"

---

18 The term in Nahuatl is *tlapanahuiya*, which is used in superlative phrases, indicating that what is at work is a comparative evaluation. This is one way that the Nahuas addressed the topic of preferences and the best life.

14. Instead you will say this: "Perhaps you are overly proud, perhaps our Lord has already uplifted your face in some matter,[19] because of those whom you first laughed at, those whom you mocked?"

And you should not mock people, you should not spit on people, you should neither urinate nor wipe your hands on people, and you should not make people consume anything but what is edible or drinkable.[20] And you should not make people consume drinks that are not good. You should not make mud near people, and that which is not wholesome you should not make people eat, nor should you make them drink that which is not potable, lest you offend our Lord, lest you reach even to His hair and head,[21] for they are quite respectable creatures of God.

15. And if you make fun of people, like this, you will not come out human.[22] With chili, with smoke you will see the earth.[23] When you die, you will enter the space next to your urine, your feces;[24] then will you roast your lip, your tongue.[25] And if you respect the chil-

---

19 Meaning that the Lord "has made you renowned in some matter."

20 The spitting, urinating, and wiping of hands may be literal, but it functions metaphorically too to indicate ways of disrespecting people. The discussion of edibility here turns on the word *qua*, to "eat," which is used in the word *qualli*, normatively "good."

21 Meaning, "lest you disrespect him."

22 A more fluid way to render this phrase might be "considered human." The difficulty with that choice is philosophical, since other-regarding dimensions aren't necessarily implied in the Nahuatl expression. I have thus rendered the point with exceptional literalness.

23 Meaning that "everything will become dark," which is a way of saying that you will suffer.

24 Meaning, roughly, that "you will be disowned and mocked."

25 Meaning that "you will receive punishment."

dren of God, only peacefully, only gently will you die. Live then in peace, going gently; do not walk like a fool, do not walk panting.

With this knowledge, somewhere you will stumble upon, with this knowledge you will meet, with an old man or an old woman, or a sick person, or a child, and there will be no excuse. Or somewhere something will be done, something will be said, something will be expressed, and thus prepared you will not hinder people, you will not mislead them, you will not afflict, you will not trouble them by reason of your ignorance.

16. And do not somewhere disorient someone, do not somewhere push people, do not repel them, for that is how you will smear yourself with urine, feces. And do not anywhere speak without consideration. Do not best people with your words and so cut off their speech. Do not talk unkindly to people, do not make them forget or fail to conserve those words which are good.[26] And if it is the elders who are speaking incorrectly, you should examine well whether you will correct them. If it is not your time to speak, you will not speak, you will not say anything, you will only be silent. And if it is also your occasion to speak or to be questioned, you should only speak this way: uprightly, absent falsehoods, and you will murmur against no one. You should make your word judicious in responding, not as a fool, nor as proud. In speaking, in answering, let your words fall only with nobility. Thus, you will be honored.

17. And beware of vain words, of jocular words, for they are vicious,[27] for they only defame people, make people vicious. They are not serenely upright. They bring people to rocky ground. They

---

26 In this case, it is helpful to recall that *tlahtolli*, "word" or "words," is also a complete thought, idea, or notion. In this case, the instruction is to refrain from persuading others to abandon good teachings.

27 Literally, "not good and right."

throw them into the river, into the cliff, into the snare for hunting, into the noose.[28] They make people suffer the stick and stone. And take care remaining in the market or at the river. On the way don't stop, don't sit down. For the owlman is there, lives there, has his great drinking trough, his feeding trough there.[29] He is another's woman, he is another's slave, another's property, another's foreign goods, another's skirt and blouse.[30]

18. And do not always seek, desire, want to look good. Do not always be combing your hair, nor always looking at yourself in the mirror; do not always get dressed up, adorn yourself; do not always desire fine adornment because that is how the owlman captures people. Thus, he poisons, gives jimsonweed to his people. For on that path[31] there your capture is no longer obvious. Somewhere your adornment, your dressing thus will throw you into the water, throw you off the cliff. Or somewhere the owlman will strike you, beat you with someone else's skirt and blouse.[32] And so that you will not be taken for a knave, when you go on the road, you should look not at one place and then another. You should only strive ahead on the march. You should not go clapping your hands, nor zigzagging on the road. You should not go being carried on the shoulders of others, nor lean on them. You should not go holding people's hands, nor go shaking your head presumptuously. You should not go making jokes, nor looking at people's faces. You should not go fre-

---

28 These are all ways of saying that they introduce people to dangerous straits.

29 See the descriptions of the owlman in part II.

30 Meaning, "another's wife."

31 The Nahuatl term here is *oncan*, literally meaning "over there." This is a spatial and temporal metaphor shading into a hypothetical situation.

32 Meaning that he "will cause you to commit adultery."

quently passing people, nor placing yourself in front others—if you were not ordered to do so.

19. And even if you are ordered to go to the front, then, perhaps you should say with insistence, you should ask yourself, do you have enough experience? It will be well, if perhaps again, if perhaps a second time you respond that you will not go to the front. And even if you go ahead of some people, you should not then hastily overtake them. You should still stop, and you should still wait for the place to be given to you.

And whenever there is an exit,[33] you should not go out first. If there are those who surpass you, they should go out first. At the entrance, you should not go in first. They, those who surpass you, should go in first. They too should be ahead when it is time to sit down. And when it is time to stand up, they should be first.

20. And when they speak, they should begin. You should not suddenly go out before them, you should not thoughtlessly take from them their preeminence, their fatherhood, if our Lord has not chosen you. And if you do not work according to their commission from Him, in whatever you do, you will incur sins.[34] And when the people of the earth see you, those who are experienced, the well-educated, the well-edified, then they will shame you, for they will know your ill-bred way of speaking.

21. They also should eat, should drink first. And you should not then, in anticipation, also desire the drink and food. You should still seek penance, humility. Then you should take the clear water, and you should wash people's hands, you should wash their mouths. If you are

---

33 That is, an exit from a home or some other edifice.

34 The context is sufficiently Christian that *tlatlacolli* is here rendered "sins," rather than "errors" or "harms."

of lineage, you should not leave your stripe, your lordship, your greatness on the wrong path.[35] Let not the jades and turquoises that fill your hands be scattered. Only in this way, with the help of *Dios*, may you be worthy.

22. If you are told later how much is needed,[36] you should not become angry. Alternatively, if you were given nothing, you should not be envious, you should not hate others, you should not leave your friends. Perhaps this is how our Lord wills it, perhaps this is how He makes you worthy. And if because of this loss of funds, you are envious, if because of this you speak with malice, then it will be seen that you are not the beloved son of *Dios*. Perhaps even a little of what you deserve will be given to you, but if you offend Him, you will come away with nothing.

23. And do not long for, do not desire the skirt and blouse who defames, debases, defiles, dirties, vitiates men.[37] Do not make your heart your mother and your father. Nor are you to make your mother and your father the scattered ashes, the crossroads.[38] For thus you will go to the head and hair of our Lord.[39] Grow strong as a slave, work before Him, work beside Him, for you are still a drop of water, a sprig of parsley, barely an ear, a sprout of corn.[40] Even though you are like

---

35 Literally, "you should not leave your greatness over there." In short, that lineage in no way excepts you from the obligation to treat others in this way.

36 Likely by way of tithing. This paragraph is probably a Christian interpolation.

37 Meaning, probably, a pleasure woman, as she is not to be desired "for long." Desiring a married woman in these discourses is expressly prohibited. See part II for a description of the pleasure woman.

38 See the gloss on these common sayings in the *Florentine Codex*, vol. 6, ch. 43, p. 247.

39 Meaning, "you will be disrespectful to Him."

40 Meaning, "you are both dear and still immature, inexperienced." In these lines diminutives are attached to all the nouns, which have had to be rendered as "drop of water" and so on, rather than the literal "small water."

a shard of jade, a bit of turquoise, a tiny quetzal plume, be not proud of yourself. Neither exalt yourself nor grandstand.

24. Where will your woman[41] go? For there is greenery, there are shoots, there are sprouts of corn, gleanings, in the earth. Let us not be anxious, even beside Him, beside our Lord. Enter, for He is still gentle. How will it be tomorrow, how will it be the day after tomorrow? Perhaps, already here, the disease and pestilence come rising to take you, to catch you. If you want to come near to a skirt, a blouse, you should tell us your mothers, your fathers. You should not just propose it, you should not just say it because you have a mother, you have a father;[42] but also because you are carried, you are borne on others' backs.[43]

25. And neither anywhere should you throw yourself in the coffer, in the reed chest of other people, nor should you throw yourself in their vessel, in their container,[44] because by doing so you will go, you will enter the wrong path.[45] And do not dedicate yourself to playing patolli,[46] to vain things, for there you will encounter the dangerous, the heavy. Perhaps somewhere, because you have stolen, you will be ashamed. In the marketplace people will shout about you. And then,

---

41 This is the difrasismo typically rendered as "skirt and blouse."

42 Meaning, "you should take them into the ambit of your consideration when deciding."

43 Meaning, "you are under the protection of others, your parents, family, and community."

44 Meaning, "you shouldn't meddle in other people's intimate affairs."

45 Literally, "you will also enter there."

46 Following Alonso de Molina's translation in his Vocabulario (2001), this is a game of dice, or more generally one of fortune. Following that approach, this is an admonition against gambling. Patolli was also a common enough board game, in which case the admonition might be against frivolity.

to whom will you give honor, if I who am your mother, your father, will be ashamed of you before others? It is enough for virtue[47] that you take care of worldly things. Work, labor, gather wood, till the ground, sow cactuses, plant magueys. It is from that which you will drink, eat, dress. With that it is enough for you to stand, for you to live. Acting thus you will be mentioned, you will be honored. In that way, by your water, by your food, will your relatives know you.

26. Maybe at some point you will hold on to a skirt and blouse,[48] what will she eat, what will she drink? Will she dine on air? For we are the relief, we are the remedy, we who are eagles and ocelots.[49] Should one or two necklaces, quetzal plumes, fall from her belly, from her breast,[50] what will they drink, what will they eat?

It is difficult to live like this on earth. It is hard, it is heavy for us, we who are commoners, we who do not arrive, who do not rise, who do not come to show ourselves. A modicum of sand, of maguey fibers, just a little bit, will be suspended on our thigh, on our hip, on our neck.[51] Meager too are what we will see, what we will eat, our maintenance, our sustenance.

27. Because much is at stake, because much grows that makes people sick, that torments them, that is arduous, that causes fear. Thus He made you grow, He strengthened you, that you might put forth branches, that you might develop. For my shoulders, my back, were much exhausted in seeking, in delivering what you drank, what you ate.

---

47 Literally, "it is already good, already right."
48 Meaning, "you will be married."
49 Meaning, "we, brave men, have an obligation to protect and sustain our wives."
50 Literally, "her belly, her throat."
51 Meaning, "We who are possessors of very little."

Moreover, I have placed a little fiber of maguey next to you,[52] because in the market, because among the merchandise I peddled[53] wood, a grain of salt, a bit of chili. And I have tilled the earth for others, I have gathered them firewood. I have carried others' staffs, I have supported their scepters.[54] In that way I filled other people's hands with a fistful of stale corn, when I had need for a little bit of grain, so that your small body would sprout, would warm. I did not abandon you. I did not forsake you. I cried much for you; I was sad. Yet, I did nothing to ruin your reputation.[55] At no time from people's bags, at no time from their coffers, in no place from their pots did I take, did I collect, to make you grow, to raise you up. Because the character of the eagle and ocelot has matured, has grown well in me. So that I shall leave you next to and beside the people only with peace and calm.

28. And beware of gossip and rumor,[56] for that is not so virtuous.[57] Nobody can in that way be, can in that way live next to and besides people. That only takes people down, only drags them into the urine and excrement. It suffices for virtue[58] if the good word—that which is well said, the well-exposed, the one that does not cause harm— were said, were expressed, before you. If you repeat it, do not exaggerate,

---

52 Meaning, "I have given you a little of what little I have achieved."

53 This is from *nentlamachtia*, which, when transitive, means to "afflict anguish on another." Metaphorically, he has afflicted his wares on others.

54 I find Silva Galeana's gloss on this phrase for his Spanish translation puzzling. It seems to me that the father is saying that he aided those who were charged with governance or the judiciary in some capacity.

55 More literally, "I did not put you in urine, in excrement."

56 More literally, "the saliva, the drool."

57 More literally, "it is not so right, so good."

58 This is the *difrasismo* "*qualli, yectli*" with "*ye*" translated as marking sufficiency.

do not embellish it. Otherwise, you will make it unequal to what was relayed to you. Only as much as you have heard, all of it, should you express to others, so that you do not cause harm.

29. If something risky is said, is done, in front of you, then you should not afterward say it, you should not then express it, you should not expose it. And even if someone asks you to make it known to them, to say it, or if someone asks you, because you were present when it was said, when it was done, you should not say it, you should not uncover it, because who knows? Will you be torn in half like a sprout, like an ear of corn? Will they peer within you as they do a coffer, a chest if your interior is well closed, if your intestines are well sealed up?

30. Let someone else say it, let someone else present it, let someone else take charge. You should not say it, you should not present it. If you do take charge, in order that you do not come across what is dangerous, what is heavy, what frightens people, then you should not defame anyone.[59] For unless you have not spoken as one who acts thus, expresses it thus, you will be harmed because there[60] you will suffer much, you will be ashamed, your reputation will be torn.[61]

31. And if you have not acted thus, as *Dios* wills, if you have not drunk or eaten what there is for people to drink, to eat, you will indeed be snared, you will be ruined, you will be broken on the earth or in the Land of the Dead.[62] Because of that nothing will be given to

---

59 More literally, "you should not put out feces, excrement."

60 The "there / *oncan*" meaning "there, then" shades into the hypothetical position of the person.

61 Literally, "lips will be torn," but *tenyotl*, meaning "reputation" or "fame," is derived from *tentli*, "lips."

62 *Mictlan*, is the region of the dead, the underearth. It was not, in preconquest

you, because of that nothing will be shown to you. You will be culpable for what happens to your face, to your heart.[63]

32.   And beware of talk concerning other people. Do not go about as a goldfinch, an amphisbaena.[64] Nowhere, amid or among people,[65] go about lying down.[66] Nowhere go about disturbing the people, do not confront the people, do not stir them up like pots, like pans. Do not divide the people, do not make them turn away from one another. In that way, perhaps, the saucepot, the basket, can persist. In that way, perhaps the *atole* and the food that makes one grow can be drunk, can be eaten. Perhaps the reed mat and seat[67] can survive. Perhaps flowers, tobacco can be given. Also throw away from yourself what is vicious, the dust and filth.[68] Do not damage, defile the reed mat and seat, public camaraderie and reciprocity, peace and prosperity. For, if you do that, you will not come out as human. That is how you will sometime pay.

---

views, a place of torment for those who were wicked in life. Its presence in this statement, then, looks to be an interpolation.

63 This phrase, "face and heart / *ixtli yollotl*," is the *difrasismo* for your character.

64 The following comparisons are to a variety of animals. The goldfinch, *chiquimoli* in Nahuatl, is figuratively a person who goes about chirping a lot, a gossip. The amphisbaena, from the Nahuatl *maquizcoatl*, is a mythical two-headed serpent, and so figuratively represents a slanderer.

65 The Nahuatl term for intersection here is *te-nepantla*, literally a space filled up with the joining of people.

66 Meaning that "you shouldn't cause trouble."

67 This is the *difrasismo* for the king, the throne, authority, organized rule, the rule of law. *Atole*, incidentally, is a corn-based beverage, sometimes mixed with chocolate.

68 The term "vicious" here is the *difrasismo* "in ahqualli, in ahyectli." Appended to the phrase are the contact era terms *in teuhtli, in tlahzolli*, here translated as "dust and filth."

33. If someone sends you somewhere, and if you are reprimanded there or someone speaks behind the back of the one who sent you, you should not become angry. Not on your lips, not in your mouth, will what happened to you, what made you suffer for having gone, come forth. And when you have returned, if the one who sent you then asks you, if he says to you, "How did it go where you went?" you should answer him gently, with good words. You should not pant, you should not then tell him what afflicted you, or of he who thus came to rebuke him, who spoke behind his back. You should not then uncover it to him. For if you then tell him so, if you then reveal it to him, perhaps you will then set them at odds, you will then inflame them. Maybe then they will quarrel, they will kill each other. And you, as an inciter, will you be happy, will your heart be right? Perhaps even then you will say: "I should not have said this so that they would not quarrel." If thus you speak, will you then be relieved? Will you then be right? For you are a gossip, for you are a slanderer. Was it only by virtue that you have come to be afflicted, or in what manner have you reviewed what transpires? Not with your envy, not with your anger should you come to reveal it, should you come to say it. That way you will only make your song and word good. For these reasons it is better that you are loved in that manner. That way you will be able to make your life next to and besides the people.

34. Nowhere with someone else's skirt and blouse should you hit yourself or hurt yourself.[69] Quite calmly, little by little, go along seeing and comprehending. One does not live twice on the earth. Only very little, only for a brief time does one come to feel the warmth thanks to our Lord. Only in that way does one emerge onto the earth. Because if it were not that way, only when the heart of *Dios* allows, He

---

69 Meaning, effectively, "do not commit adultery with someone else's wife."

would instead correct us and judge us. Moreover, He would reciprocate according to our works, according to our merit, that of which we are worthy.[70]

And do not take something thoughtlessly, nor thoughtlessly crave it. Do not unreflectively want to outdo people, nor to surpass them in what is not your due, in what is not your desert, in what is not your lot; do not so get it, do not so take it. For He alone, our Lord, *Dios*, makes people, for He alone gives this, bestows this on each one. For what you will get, what will belong to your life is your due, your desert, your lot. When our Lord grants you something, then on that will you be, will you stand, will you live. And you will be unable to live well on your lot unless you are prudent, unless you live frugally.[71] In this way what you deserve will grow, for so will our Lord do unto you. And if you just accept your lot, on account of that no one will speak of it, no one will be afflicted by it, because it is your property, because it is your desert, because it is your gift. And if without reflection you take what you do not deserve, what is not your gift, then you will be troubled by this, you will be ashamed, and you will be distressed before our Lord.

35. And if someone talks to you, you should not be drawing pictures on the ground, you should not be playing with something, you should not be beating your feet, you should not be wiggling them, you should not be rubbing them, you should not be nibbling your

---

70 Recall that in the Christian context, because we are sinners, God's reciprocation would be punishment. We do not merit salvation, but rather achieve it, ultimately, by God's grace.

71 The terms used here are not the standard ones and have a slightly different meaning. "You are prudent" translates *timihmatini*, which turns on know-how, *imati*, not theoretical wisdom. "Frugally" translates *ycnotlacayotl*, which is variously the state of being an orphan, misery, or poverty. It is hyperbole for frugality.

clothes, you should not be spitting, you should not be looking this way and that, you should not be getting up in haste, you should not be lying down, you should not be scratching yourself.

These things I have warned you, if you wrongly act thus, you will then appear as a quite wicked person. On that path[72] your face, your heart shall not be, for you will[73] then be one who leaves yourself behind thoroughly. Because by your own accord your due, your desert will be mind-altering herbs. You will drink pulque, eat the hallucinating mushroom. In that way you will become drunk. In that way you will be ruined. In that way you will no longer understand. You will throw yourself on embers, into the skillet's fire, into the river, into the ravine. You will enter into the hunter's trap and cord; so you will no longer understand; so you will stumble into the stick and stone, the excrement, the feces;[74] so you will live in front of and on top of people; so you will run away, you will become a savage; so you will find the way of the rabbit, of the deer; so you will go into the forest, into the grass, if you do not take, if you do not receive,[75] what belongs to your mothers, your fathers, if you do not want to listen to what keeps you on your feet, what allows you to live. In that case, everything has already been said and done, it has been vitiated. Because you will only fall. Because only into the clutches of a coyote, of a beast, will you go.

36. Do not for some reason come to be displeased with what is in the past, what in vain transpired, arose for you. Because in truth you did not receive, you did not make the weeping, the tears your

---

72 Literally, "for over there." The hypothetical eventuality, a possible world, is expressed spatially in Nahuatl.

73 Literally, "are then." The indicative is used here to express maximal certitude.

74 Meaning "infamy."

75 The Nahuatl uses two different terms for "take" in this phrase. Throughout the work, they are rendered "take" and "receive," since this is more idiomatic in English.

own. And because in truth you did not bring the scorpion, the nettle,[76] close to you when it was given to you as food, because you only threw it away, you pushed it away with your hand, you despised it. In that way you could have educated yourself, you could have observed. But you chalked them up only to the stick and stone.[77]

And you do not place on your face, on yourself, that of which *Dios* has made you worthy. If in that way your corrupt yourself, if thus you mock others, you will eat yourself, you will consume yourself along with people. And in that way you will afflict, thus you will displease our Lord, who perhaps would still have set you on high.

37. And when you eat, do not look at people in disgust. Do not leave food for people in anger. To him who comes to you, you should give something, even if it is just a bit of what you have earned, otherwise he might go away hungry. If you eat with someone, do not let the morsel get stuck in your throat, so that you choke, trip your tongue over your food. And you should not finish first, you should finish after the other has.

And if you live next to someone, you should take care not to set his house on fire. You should put things in order, you should sweep. In that way you will stand, so you will live. In that way you will drink, you will eat next to and beside people. Because if you were only to make things bent or dirty, you will not long remain.

38. If you live well, if you do well what I tell you, then, when you are seen, the stick and stone will be directed to the one who does not live well, to the one who does not obey his father, his mother.

---

76 Meaning, "you did not accept hard lessons."

77 Meaning that they became only bad consequences, rather than life lessons from which you might have learned.

And now, that is all. I, your mother, your father, am retiring. In this way I give you encouragement, thus I strengthen you, so I put white varnish on you, thus I deck you with feathers.[78] Do not anywhere throw away, do not anywhere cast away these lessons. This is now all that you must understand.[79] May it be an inspiration to you, may it remind you of the Lord, our Lord, *Dios*.

---

78 Meaning, "I make you worthy."

79 This is typically the last line of a discourse. The following sentence is likely a later Christian interpolation.

Answer in which the son in this way replies to his father

39. My father, you have granted your heart to me, you have been kind to me. I am your necklace, your quetzal plume.[1] Will I get, will I appropriate one lip, one mouth,[2] that which comes out, which falls out, spills out, and scatters from your entrails, from your throat? In this way you fulfill your duty to me—I who am your necklace and quetzal plume. So, I will not be angry. Perhaps I have once done something bad, I have done what is vicious.[3] In that case, you will not be reproached, my father.

40. I am still a little boy, a young child, I still stir the earth, I am still playing with pots; I still play with my urine, with my feces, I still stir my drool, my snot, in my hands. Because not much yet do I see, do I hear; not much I have grown. I do not yet have practical wisdom.[4]

Where indeed will you send me? For you are my mother, my father, and I your blood and color. For one lip, one mouth come forth, fall forth from you who are my mother, my father. Will you forsake me? Only when I cannot make your word mine, when I cannot appropriate it, then you will forsake me.

---

1 This is a *difrasismo* for child.

2 This is a *difrasismo* for a thought or doctrine—roughly what passes through the breach in one's lips.

3 This is the negative form of the *difrasismo* "*qualli, yectli.*"

4 The term at stake uses "*imati*" as part of a larger compound term.

41. And now that is all. So, I return your breath,[5] your word, a lip, a stammering mouth. It is covered in dirt, broken. It is a boy's word, a child's word, the single lip, the single mouth that does not yet come out well, that does not yet fall well. Take thy seat, O Father mine.

---

5 The term here is *ihiyotl*, which is one of the three principle animating forces in a person's body. It is, in the last paragraphs of this work (cf. par. 201–2), appropriated into a Christian context, though it here means something closer to vital force.

Words of exhortation by which the mother thus speaks, instructs her daughter

42. Now my little girl, little lovebird, little woman, you have life, you have been born, you have come out, you have fallen from my breast, from my bosom. Because your father, your Lord, has forged you, because he has molded you, he made you, he formed you, little one. May you not go suffering on the earth. How will you live among the people, with the people? For in dangerous places, in dreadful places, one lives with great difficulty. In that way there is hardship on the earth, so that people's faces and hearts,[1] their shoulders and backs, their elbows and knees, are thus entirely used up. In that way, our Lord grants people a little, makes them deserving of their fame, their honor, their heat, their warmth, their sweetness, their savoriness.

43. But concerning you, who are my necklace and quetzal plume, abandon yourself not, nor waste yourself, nor leave yourself behind. Damage not your face and heart, nor with them your shoulder, your back, your elbow, and your knee when you set yourself to sweep, to clean, set yourself up to wash the hands, the face, the mouth of others. Moreover, place yourself next to the water and metate.[2] Take up well, grasp the molcajete, the basket, and place and separate them well before and beside the people.

---

1 This is the *difrasismo* "*ixtli, yollotl*," meaning "character."

2 The water and metate stand metonymically for the work of women in Nahua culture. The sentence means, then, that you should observe the duties of your social role as a woman.

Do not go seeking discussion, and not without consideration should you offer it. Only calmly, gently, should you reveal your word. And you should not go along as a fool, go along panting, go laughing. You should not go looking in front of you, nor across. You should not go following people with your eyes, nor look people right in the face. You should only go straight ahead. You should only go looking straight ahead when you address people or go out before them or when you meet them.[3] In that way you will have fame, honor. So, no one will turn you away, no one will disturb you. Thus, only following the middle way is there community and honor.[4]

44. And she who follows the middle way sings well, speaks well, converses well, answers well, makes requests well. One's word is not something that can be bought. Do not become someone mute or foolish. And take charge of the spindle, the weaving tablet. Labor, that which elevates, what makes one noble, what makes one deserving, even what lies in the painted books, the model, the color red,[5] rise from the earth like a fragrance. In that way you will live well next to and beside the people. In that way you will, at some point, deserve a bit of *atole*, a folded tortilla, some greens, some cactus. And at some point, a few grains, some stale corn, will hang from your hip, from your chest, so that your body will be heated up and warmed. In this way you will thank our Lord for His mercy with the people, His benevolence with the people.

---

3 In essence, keep your eyes down, except with greeting or speaking with people, as a sign of respect.

4 The "middle way" is *nepantla* in Nahuatl.

5 This phrase, "what lies in the painted books, the model, the color red," is an extended metaphor for "what makes one wise."

45. And do not take sleeping and lying down as sweet and savory.[6] And do not vainly follow the day and night. That is vicious[7] since it makes people acquire, it makes them desire, it teaches them what is bad, what is done from sloth. In order that somewhere you might be[8] next to and beside people, virtue requires that you know, that you carry on your back, that you lead your life bearing what is virtuous. What you should do, what you should bear on your back is what it is possible to do, what is bearable, whether that is by the side of our Lord, or what we, the deserving ones, need.

46. And if you are called, not twice, not three times, not many times should you be called, but only once; then you should stand up with haste so that you do not provoke anger, so that none are troubled by your disobedience. If anything is said to you, is communicated to you, is commanded at you, then you should hear it well, you should put it in your heart[9] so that you will not forget it. And you should carry it out well, not change it much,[10] nor disdain it, nor reject it, nor snub the word. For if you cannot do it, calmly and quietly, make that clear. So, no longer mock, make fun of people because our Lord sees you. Only, in truth, should you mention what you cannot do.

47. Or if you were not called, if another person is spoken to and does not want to stand up quickly, and perhaps does not want

---

6 Meaning, "don't be lazy."

7 This is the *difrasismo* "*qualli, yectli*" in negated form.

8 The grammar in Nahuatl is clear that what follows concerns the conditions for the possibility of "being" in a certain way—namely, living harmoniously among other people.

9 More literally, you should en-heart it. This is one of the metaphors used for habituation.

10 Literally, "give it many turns."

to listen, does not want to do what he has been told, what he has been commanded, then you will quickly stand up, listen to the word, and do what the other person should do. For in truth, it is better if you are loved in that way, for doing this.

And if anyone should say something to you, concerning what is necessary for your heart, or that by which one lives well, by which one stands on the earth, you should comprehend it, take it, and make it part of your life. For if you do not comprehend it, if you do not take it, if you do not obey, then many omens, unusual things, will be against you because living like this you will not be esteemed on earth.

48. And bow, lower your head before people, next to and beside the people be respectful, be fearful of them. Not in front of and on top of the people are you to go.[11] Live with tranquility, with calm. Love the people, beg of them, be benevolent to them. At some point,[12] give others a little something. Look not at people with disdain and be not greedy.

And be not one sided, or scrutinize people for their wealth when our Lord gives it to someone. Do not make someone suffer, do not treat them that way. Do not mock someone, for then you will be afflicted. And beware of playing with dung.[13] Take not as mother, as father the ashes, the crossroads.[14]

---

11 This is a *difrasismo* meaning not to disrespect or lose respect for people.

12 Literally, "somewhere." This is an example of the way in which spatial terms take on what in English has temporal significance.

13 This is a metaphorical way of stating "Avoid involving yourself in disrespectful affairs."

14 This is a *difrasismo* meaning that the daughter is not to put her parents or family in danger or into disrepute.

49. By your own accord, eat not your hand or foot.[15] Make not your mother, your father a whim,[16] for thus you will emerge, for thus you will wear out, you will become debased, you will be covered with black. And you will also thus shame us even when you are as water, as food,[17] because just by your own accord, you still came to be mixed up in what is vicious.[18]

And do not make friends with liars, with thieves, with pleasure women, with busybodies, with the slothful, so that they do not criticize you, do not bewitch you. Just dedicate yourself at home to what you are going to do. Do not go outside, and do not put yourself in the market, in the river, on the road, in a vicious place. There is what disfigures, what stains, what endangers, what causes affliction, what makes people like animals, what is not good, what is wrong, what does not merely approximate the hallucinogenic herbs, what is in excess, what frightens greatly, what leaves people without tranquility, what throws them into what is turbulent.

50. And if you somewhere meet a person, a wicked man, if he makes fun of you, do not laugh at him. Just keep silent, you should see nothing, you should deduce nothing from his word, from his joke. You should remember nothing of that, of what dishonors people, of what defiles people, of wrongs.[19]

If he were to follow you, if he were to say something behind your back,

---

15 Meaning, "do not harm yourself."

16 Meaning, "do not treat them and their welfare lightly."

17 Meaning, "even if you are indispensable to us."

18 This is the *difrasismo* "*ahqualli, ahyectli.*"

19 In Nahuatl this is simply *tlahtlacolli.* In the Christian contexts of the last passages, it is translated as "sin."

if he were to do something, you should not get entangled, you should not look at him out of the corner of your eye. You should not say something to him, so that you do not provoke him, so that you do not excite the wicked one. Because if you do not answer him, that is the only way he will leave you alone. You will just be busily on your way. You should not chew gum either.[20]

And do not go thoughtlessly into people's houses, for rumors will be imputed to you.[21] If, when you enter the house of your relatives, you wake them up, you should respect them so that nothing bad will happen to you. You should not go around laughing, you should be considerate of them, you should respect your relatives.

51. With haste you should take the spindle and weaving board, the water and metate, the molcajete and basket. You should not merely go about carrying things, nor fill your hands with them. And when you marry someone who is an eagle, ocelot, do not go in front of and on top of him.[22] When he asks you a question, goes imposing things[23] on you, warns you, you should obey him well, you should hear his word with joy. Not later should you suffer to receive his word angrily, nor then should you be annoyed, nor become a back-talker, nor turn against him. If something bothers you, in that case you should not also remind him of it, nor make fun of him for it, nor should you be covetous, though he be a humble person.

---

20 Chewing gum was associated with the activities of pleasure women.

21 Literally, "something will be imputed to you there." The idea is that by entering others' houses, people may suspect illicit sexual relations to have occurred.

22 Meaning that you should not "lose respect for him."

23 More colloquially (and less accurately philosophically), "imposing his will on you."

52. If he lives thanks to you, because he is under your protection, you should place him under your protection, but you should not count yourself as an eagle, as an ocelot. You should not only do carelessly what he entrusts to you, in order that you may not offend our Lord and He may not give you sufferings. Only gently, only calmly, shall you tell him what troubles you. Not in front of people, beside people should you shame him.[24] For if you shame him, then so your heart, your bowels, that which you make live before people,[25] you drag down.

And if someone bothers him, you should take care if he behaves incautiously, unobservantly. Addressing your husband, you should tell him how he will stand, how he will live upon the earth. And you should take care for what he drinks, and what he eats, or generally if anything is heated in your house, what is warmed on your hearth, in your home.

53. And you should protect your farming beds, your sowing fields. And you should take good care of your workers. Moreover, you should guard well the coffer, the reed chest, close well the pots and bowls.[26] Do not degrade yourself all on your own, nor crumble on your own accord, nor scatter yourself by only going out, by only running about.[27] You will never see your pots and bowls, nor your home, nor your house, if you so live.

And if you are to have your belongings, your property, you should not waste them, not without consideration should you bring them to market. Thus, He will not be afflicted, because you will help Him, because

---

24 This means "do not publicly act to shame or bring him shame." Both cases are possible given the transitive nature of the Nahuatl verb.

25 Meaning your reputation.

26 Meaning that "you should manage the household finances."

27 The Nahuatl grammar here is hypothetical rather than instrumental, literally reading "if you only go out, etc." Such constructions fare poorly in English.

you will guard what is yours thanks to our Lord. You will warm yourselves a little, you will heat your bodies, so that you will leave what is
yours, to your children, to your grandchildren.

54. If thus you act to do these things, about which I have told you, about which I have edified you, then truly you will live well, with the favor of and beside the people. Thus, I who am an old man, I who am an old woman, I who teach, I who educate, fulfill my duty to you. For nothing will turn deceitful if you get this word, if you listen to it, if you take it, if you place it in your belly, in your throat. It will be your gift, it will be your desert, that by which you will live. The good song, the good word must settle in, because if you do not receive it, then what is wrong will have happened, transpired. In vain will you perish dread-fully. In vain will you see scandals transpire,[28] little girl, my little daughter, if you do not receive, if you do not get that which is the wisdom of motherhood and fatherhood, if only behind you and in back of you, you hurl and dash what guides you, what leads you.

---

28 Literally, "what will be your head's scandal."

The daughter's response to her mother and her thanks for the talk and edification

55. Older sister,[1] you have shown me favor, I who am your necklace, your precious plume. Truly, where will you leave me? Where will you deliver me? Because in your belly and throat have I lived, have I been born, I, who am a young girl, a little girl. So may I take it, so may I understand from[2] you who you are my mother, my older sister, my father.

For much does your face, your heart, your body lack in compensation because that is how you raised me, on my behalf, that is how you deprived yourself. By the stove, in our home you worried[3] over me, whether you had hurt my lip, and as you lulled me. Because for my sake you quite feared that something unforeseen might happen,[4] and you had only disturbed sleep and rest. For my sake you watched well and with your hand you collected my urine and my excrement. Your dear milk, which poured into my mouth, dripped into me, spilled out, and became substantial with effort and struggle.[5]

With difficulty your milk comes to flow for that is what you now do.

---

1 The Nahuas often used kinship inversion in especially polite contexts. For example, an older man might call a boy "my uncle," or a daughter might call her mother "my sister."

2 Literally, "see in you."

3 Literally, "nodded."

4 Literally, "because of me you were afraid of something behind your back."

5 This phrase "with effort and struggle," is literally the opposite of the common *difrasismo* for tranquility, *"aihuiyan, icemele."*

On my behalf, in your womb, in your gut, misery is stuck to you. And now they are no longer your belongings, the earnings from your spindle, your weaving tablet.[6] They are what you gave me to drink, to eat so that I would come to grow a little, to add some flesh.

56. Even now you falter not in providing aid for me. Again, you tell me, you give me what makes me stand up, what makes me live. And what shall I give you in return? With what shall I appease your heart, your body? For I am still a little girl, a little child, for I still pile up the earth and play with pots, for I still make games with my urine, and my feces, for I still smear my drool, my snot on my hands, for my face and my heart are not yet mature.

Also, as the Lord wills, our Lord, perhaps it will be what I deserve, perhaps what you have told me, what you have given me, a lip, a mouth, your weeping, your tears, will be what I merit. And perhaps you will somewhere deserve a little bit of warmth and heat—the warmth and heat of our Lord. May it be my gift now that your heart has bestowed so much! Be strengthened my elder sister.

---

6 Meaning, what effort you expended in completing your work in your role as a woman. It might also mean that she literally spent the money earned selling textiles on her daughter. In both cases, this is a consequence that follows from her role as a mother.

The father's exhortation, edification by which he exhorts his son when he is still a little boy

57. My blood and color, I have forged you, given you a start. Already before you and above you I stand guard. May you not be just precious metal, since you have been forged in this way. For you still come with sleep in your eyes and you will later come to discover your face. Perhaps you are but a little bird, and you are yet to be covered with feathers, and to grow wings. Do not anywhere flutter before and above the people.[1] Only peacefully should you fly near to, next to the ceiba, the ahuehuete, lest by carelessness you at some point[2] damage them, because in that way you will hurt them. And you will come to observe that thanks to them you will have peace of mind.

58. And if you are here yet one day, two days, thanks to the Lord of the Near and the Nigh, I see before you and above you, I will even make you eat the jade, the turquoise,[3] so that you do not follow the rabbit, the deer, so that somewhere you do not fall into a ravine and remain entangled there. For only in this way will you follow the straight path, the one followed by those who on earth are coffers and reed chests,[4] who are quite respectful and work well with others, who are trusted and well within them is placed the necklace, the quetzal plume,

---

1 Meaning, "don't be disrespectful of people."

2 Literally, "somewhere."

3 Meaning, "I will instill in you what is edifying."

4 Meaning, "those who guard the good words well." See also *Florentine Codex*, vol. 6, ch. 43, p. 247.

the jade. And where now does it come, where will it yet emerge, what is in your belly, in your ribs?

59. And you who are my heart, who are part of my body, of what I give you to eat, that which is eaten here on earth, you must know that it is its precious food, bring it close to you. Make yourself not as a stone, for you know that if a stone is hard, it takes more than one time to break it. And you, be not called many times, for the heart within you is the one *Dios* has given you. Thank him for it. That is all that I, your mother, your father, bind in your breast and throat.

The exhortation, edification in which the father exhorts and educates his son

60. My necklace, my quetzal plume, as precious metal is forged, as jade is pierced, so you have been forged, so you have been pierced. With necklaces, quetzal plumes I am endowed. One lip, two lips I here wish to bind on your ears. Perhaps, perhaps in this way, perhaps not, perhaps I'll just stutter, I'm an old man, an old woman. Bring my words to your belly, your throat only in this way. You, my foot, my hand,[1] are distressed. You are a necklace, quetzal plume, you are a tail and wing.[2] Whence comes yet a lip, a mouth?[3] I shall make you eat, make you swallow the jade so that you are not an empty coffer or reed chest.[4] Whence do they still come? Within you will the jade, the turquoise, that which is hidden, that which is kept be concealed.[5]

61. And now you have observed, you have understood, you yourself ought not make people walk on tiptoe. And they are distressed, those who scatter you, those who disseminated you into the world.[6] Perhaps again they, the face and heart of the people, will come to

---

1 Meaning that "you are my extension, my legacy."

2 The *difrasismo* "tail, wing" includes in its meaning the sense that "you are of the common people."

3 Meaning, effectively, "will you be the one receiving the advice?"

4 The Nahuatl literally reads, "not just a coffer, a reed chest."

5 The Nahuatl is in the active voice without a clearly identified third-person-singular agent.

6 In the Nahuatl, "into the world" is not present. I have added it for the sake of clarity.

make you eat, to make you drink what is sweet, savory? And moreover, say what the old man, the old woman, says: Why is this not something? For I only hold those who are your hands, your feet.[7] Perhaps in this way, perhaps not, I will be your mother, your father. Is this how you will throw me down, how you will kick me, I who am your mother, I who am your father? You who are of jade, of a quetzal plume, live peacefully, calmly thanks to the Lord of the Near and the Nigh. Spend your life not by going to one place and the next without purpose, going along like a clown. The One by Whom We Live will make you remain here perhaps one day, perhaps two days.

62. And you know that the deer, when pursued, is frightened, he does not know that he is going to fall into the trap where he will die. And you, are you a deer who does not know where it is going? Because you have been shown the path that you should follow, and if you lose it, then it will have been by your own accord that you consumed it. Just like the fruit tree that no longer blooms, that no longer buds— it only blooms and buds if it withstands the frost—then it withers and dries up. And you, if you no longer bloom, if you no longer bud, when it is time for blooming, when it is time for buds to grow, then it is because of your accord that you have hurled yourself into the mouth of the wild beasts.

63. Is it perhaps with gentility, with calm that one lives on earth? This is all that I bring to you, to your dear hand, to your dear foot. Let it be so with your hand, your face, your heart. Shall I for once make you eat, shall I make you drink my drool, the foam of my mouth?[8] This is all there is for you to hear, my son.

---

7 Meaning, "those who are your servants."

8 Meaning, "Will I succeed in getting you to live by my words?"

**The father's exhortation, how he speaks to his son
when he is of the age that he wants to get married**

64. My son, my boy, you have toiled, you work, you do the work of a slave, and the Lord of the Near and the Nigh, the One by Whom We Live has made you understand everything. Our Lord, *Dios*, gives you life here perhaps one day, two days. Perhaps here one day, two days he will even make you an eagle, an ocelot.[1] Perhaps in that case you are joined to the eagle, joined to the ocelot, because that is how you have been forged, because that is how you have been pierced, namely as the litter, the cord for bearing the burden.[2] Will you give luster, will you defend the nobility, their legacy, as is the characteristic of the eagle, the ocelot, so that you are as an eagle, you are as an ocelot[3] who thus walk on tiptoe?

65. My son, my boy, that is how you are, that is how you show yourself. Are you still playing with earth and pots?[4] You suffer because you are already this way. You are a mirror because you have already shown who you are. You are a flower because you have bloomed, and you are one who has accepted the way things are, one who has matured. And everything here has been said about you, for

---

1 Meaning, most directly, that "he will make you a warrior." But the passage also concerns courage, the quality typical of warriors, so that the line also means "he will give you courage."

2 Meaning that it is your role to facilitate, to hold up others.

3 Meaning, "so that you are as one who has courage." This sentence uses the *difrasismo* first to indicate a social role and then to indicate the quality of one's character.

4 This statement, expressed rhetorically as an interrogative, effectively means "you are no longer a child."

whom a meeting has been held, and here they charge you with a skirt and blouse.

66. And here everything must be hung up, the weaving tablet, the four grasses.[5] And here, do we know everything, how we must go along on the earth? Perhaps we only go in this way by probing with our feet? Who knows about tomorrow, the day after tomorrow? Perhaps even we will know, for if not, He alone, the Lord of the Near and the Nigh, will know. Might you guide yourself? Might you carry yourself? No. You are guided; you are carried.[6] Moreover, my son, my boy, where yet do you say you are going, where yet do you say you are suffering? Not in vain have the jade, the mirror been shown, have they come to be observed. And you too have shown who you are, have been seen. Before you, those who scattered you, disseminated you into the world, have observed.

67. And here be bold, benefit others. And so, here, they will speak of you, and you will be on their lips. And here also, on your behalf, they will be honored, be renowned, painted in colors.[7] And here, here they will strive like eagles. You who are jade, a quetzal plume, act beneficially for your face and heart. Forge yourself here, pierce yourself, so that here you will add flesh, here you will grow. Perhaps what I who am your mother, your father want you to do annoys you? Am I an old shield, an old club? And this, my boy, is all that I bind to your belly, on

---

5 Meaning effectively, "you should be prepared by having the tools for the job."

6 Meaning effectively, "you should not forget that your parents care for you." The "not" is implied rhetorically.

7 "Painted in colors" means made famous in a way like our contemporary "to have your name in lights."

your neck. Strengthen your hands, your feet.[8] And benefit your relatives, lest here on your face, above your person, you harm yourself. Only like this, only with negligence do I, your mother, your father, speak my boy.

---

8 Meaning, "train yourself."

Here is how the boy responds, gives something in return

68. My father, your heart has been generous. Who am I? To whom am I responsible? Am I an eagle, an ocelot? Will I thus make you forget, will I thus put you at ease if your gift penetrates my ears, the place where I am edified, like the arrow of an eagle, of an ocelot. You make me eat what is like a turquoise bracelet, rounded, a bit of jade. As your son,[1] you bind it on my wrist, my throat. You benefit me. May your face, your heart do me good, so that I may still get something from you in one day, two days. For even before you, and above you I watch.[2]

69. Where will you cast me, really? Where will you leave me, really? Perhaps in this way I am your eagle, I am your ocelot, but perhaps not? Will you get tired here, will you get discouraged, even if I am your gift, what you deserve? And if even one day, two days, the Lord of the Near and the Nigh, the One by Whom We Live, *Dios*, makes me live, will I make you live in front of and on top of the people?[3] And will I push them to the reed mat, to the seat,[4] with my foot? Have I come out a quarrelsome boy? Do I not observe before, not above others? Do you say that it is vain to know on earth? Because that is not true, it is not vain.

70. Shall we see behind us, in back of us, how the sandy, the stormy comes, which is here like a trap for people? Shall we step into the snare that catches humans? And with this will you rejoice

---

1 Literally, "as a necklace."

2 Meaning, "I have respect for you."

3 Meaning, "Will I make you to act without consideration for others?"

4 Meaning "to the throne," and so, metonymically, "to those who rule."

for me? Will you rejoice that I am your eagle, that I am your ocelot? And here, on me, will you place all your shields, your swords?[5] Here next to me will you bring the hot, the warm, and the cold, the icy, that which edifies, that which makes one see? Will I discourage your hands, your feet, so that you dash me, so that you throw me, I who am your necklace, your quetzal plume? Will I listen, will I not take into account the source of life,[6] which you place in me?

71. And here, in this way you give me, I who am stubborn, more than I deserve. You are my beloved father, and your face and your heart have delivered gifts. In this way, you have come to leave me that which is as precious as jade, as turquoise.[7] And perhaps here I may put my heart into things and become quite like a coffer, like a reed chest. Perhaps already here, within me, the necklace, the quetzal plume is placed,[8] because in truth it yet comes to me and soothes your face, your heart.

72. Therefore, you who are an old man, you who are an old woman, I kiss your hand, your foot. And still thus I go about boasting, I, your necklace, your quetzal plume, your jade, your turquoise, am a tuft of your hair, an extension of you. And even here I am still suffering, I am still passing the time. My father, your heart has been afflicted, you have done right by me.

---

5 These would not have been swords in the European sense. The Nahuatl word refers to wooden clubs or batons, though the speaker might also have in mind those with obsidian blades.

6 In the original Nahuatl: *tzihuactli, tetehuitli,* meaning "the dry, the humid," is a *difrasismo* that refers to two sacrificial objects. The metaphorical suggestion is "that which belongs to life."

7 These last terms mean "admonitions, recommendations."

8 Meaning "I have received and habituated the word, the teaching."

Here is how a father exhorts his son when he has married

73. My son, eagle and ocelot, tail and wing, perhaps here, on your wrist, on your throat, one lip, two lips, the jade that I have given you to keep will be tied? You who are obstinate, after one day, two days, I have made you worthy of something that is well deserved, well carried out. About what concerns life[1] I have been correcting you. For one day, two days, in your ears, in your heart I have been hanging these teachings, I, your father, your mother.

74. And with this perhaps it is already time, and there I, who am an old man, an old woman, will be astonished. Perhaps already now the coffer, the reed chest will be opened.[2] And perhaps already now I will see how you will accompany, how you will make the spindle and tablet for weaving follow the path.[3] Perhaps for one day, two days, she will be subject of your care. For so must you also become a mother to her. And here make her follow the path, that which should be followed, and teach her what will make her wise. Similarly, bind the jade and turquoise[4] on her wrist and throat. And on her side, on her ears, on her heart, hang them too, my son.

---

1 A *difrasismo* that means, literally, "the dry, the wet."

2 In this case, the line means, effectively "my heart will be opened."

3 This line uses a metonymic reference for the son's wife, for whom the spindle and the weaving tablet are the two principal instruments of her work as a woman. Just as the mother advises her daughter to help her husband follow the path (*ohtli*), here one witnesses the reciprocal obligation for the son.

4 Meaning, "teach her the edifying doctrines in a way that she habituates and binds them."

75. Let others esteem you.[5] For from he who instructs others to be wise is founded, is initiated how not to lose his footing if one has learned. Those who suffer, one or two of them, are those who disseminate, who scatter their spindle and weaving tablet. And here honor me, flatter me, I who am your mother, your father; let your word be virtuous,[6] and in this way respect it, honor it. Is one born twice? Does one die twice? Does one twice live on earth? For only once does one live, thanks be to our Lord, *Dios*; if not, it will be only when I am resurrected.[7]

76. Let your renown, your fame, be righteous. By your deeds, in that case, may I be a valued old man, a valued old woman. And in that way, my blood and color, I am satisfied. Let it be shown there that you are my blood, that you are my color. Let nothing become a source for our reprimand, our shame, our submission, our harm. peacefully, calmly, pass the day, the evening. And have respect, be considerate in the courtyard, the hearth, the doorway.[8] Let not the dust and filth expand. Let no bit of chili be broken in my presence, I who am an old man, an old woman, because it is quite painful, and I no longer appreciate it. And well, peacefully, calmly, accompany each other, direct yourselves together, and take for yourselves that which gives life, that which lets us abide. Take care of the working tool, the hygienic instruments. And with like care, lead her to use the spindle, the weaving tablet.[9] And, my son, my boy, my necklace, my precious feather, go showing her what is the way you should follow. That's all. That's all I put forth, what I express in your presence and to your heart.

---

5 Meaning, "be a role model for other people."

6 This is the *difrasismo "qualli, yectli."*

7 These last statements are clear interpolations.

8 Meaning, "the entire household."

9 Meaning, "make her do women's work."

Words of exhortation that the father says to his married, beloved son

77. My son, take heart. Perhaps here in a day, in a little while, you will be awaiting the stick and stone, the illness and pestilence[1] of our Lord. On His mount and water[2] you walk, shedding tears, crying, for one day, two days. Not peacefully, gently do you come to get up, to awake. Not peacefully, gently do you sleep, do you rest. With someone's favor, next to them, your bedside is filled only with your old shoes, your scepter, your carrying frame, your folded tortilla, your digging stick, your carrying rope,[3] by which our Lord brought you fame and honor. You are an eagle, you are an ocelot; it is your gift, what you deserve. You are the brave one, the singer of the people. The bricks, the mortar, the carrying frame, the scepter, the digging stick, the carrying rope—they are how you help the mount and water, the reed mat and seat. With these you educate people, you instruct them. It is with these that you are well located next to the people, that you are seated at their side. May you place your carrying frame, your scepter, your digging sticks, your carrying rope by your side.

78. Gird and twist the carrying rope well,[4] for that will sustain you, those are your greens, your nopals. Give no rest to your

---

1 These are both *difrasismos* that concern punishments and bad consequences.

2 A city in Nahua culture is literally an *altepetl* (from atl + tepetl), or water-hill.

3 The terms used here are *huictli, mecapalli,* which often form a *difrasismo* for the work carried out by commoners.

4 The carrying rope is here inferred from the context, but is not directly mentioned in the text.

forehead, to your back. Throw not your shoes, your carrying frame, or your scepter behind you.[5] Give rest not to your hands, to your feet. Acquiesce not on your face, on your heart, on your shoulders, on your back.[6] If you do so, if you acquiesce on your face, on your heart, how will you stand, how will you live next to and beside people? How will your necklaces and quetzal plumes stand, how will they live? How will the one with skirt and blouse stand, how will she live? For all these reasons, the work of servitude, of tribute, honors people; it exalts them.

79. And take care that the one with the skirt and blouse does her work with the spindle, with the weaving board, with the water, the metate. And that if one or two necklaces and quetzal plumes were born, came forth from her womb, from her throat, from the one with skirt and blouse, that she should care for them too. For these reasons correct and watch over yourself. For these reasons watch over them. Moreover, give and deliver a lip, a mouth, what is proper to a mother, a father, so that they may stand well, so that they may live well on earth— so that they may not live without respect for our Lord, so that they do not go to his head and hair,[7] so that they do not in front of and on top of the people,[8] and so that they may not bring shame to you.

80. Additionally, let not the labor of servitude, the labor of trib- ute, frighten you. For with the favor of the peoples you will secure what the children will drink, what they will eat, that with which

---

5 Meaning, effectively, "neglect not your obligations."

6 Meaning, "let not your character (face and heart) slide into indolence."

7 Meaning, so that "they do not disrespect Him."

8 Meaning, "so that they live respectfully."

you make them grow, that with what you provide for them, and even that which will hang on them.[9]

And watch out for the one with the skirt and blouse, for what will hang from her hip, from her neck.[10] And watch out for what will warm, what will give heat in your hearth, in your home. By doing that you will warm your mothers, your fathers, your uncles, your aunts, and your relatives. You will warm their hearts, their bodies a little bit. And perhaps someone will come to visit, to say hello at your house, then you should receive him inside your house. Somewhere there is a little of what the poor seek, and for this they cry. Your sustenance, your knee, your shoulder, will move them. So too will the sweetness, the salt, the taste of the chili, of the tree, of the greens, of the cactuses, and their value move them. This is how they will honor you, exalt you, thanks be to our Lord.

81. And love the people, pray to them. Live not in front of and on top of them. Only with your head bowed, your neck bent should you go acting before and beside people. With their favor is how you will be loved, how you will be obeyed. Reproach not, correct not your hand, your foot if it is already much, quite a bit, the work of servitude, of tribute that you do. Not in front of and on top of you should you put it,[11] because otherwise you will disturb, you will bother *Dios*. In that way you will provoke His anger, His wrath—that of the One by Whom We Live. In that way He will come to wield His stick, cast His stone, show His anger, His indignation, His wrath.

---

9 Meaning, quite literally, "their clothes."

10 Meaning, in a limited sense, her clothes, but more generally her material possessions.

11 Meaning, effectively, "you should not be too proud of your work and accomplishments."

82. For acting in that way you will surely be blinded, you will go along with a limp, your arm will be twisted. That is how things will be afterward, for thus you have become crazy, you have lost yourself without profit. Our Lord will have taken from you what made you prosper, what filled you with pride. It is virtuous that you obey your mothers, your fathers who guide you to undertake the labor of servitude, of tribute. For neither are they content, neither are they happy, as their hearts, their bodies are also troubled, tormented. If, then, you do not obey them, if you only move against them, if you only oppose them, if you suddenly attack them,[12] then their trouble, their torment, their anguish, their anxiety, their worry, their tribulation, will manifest[13] because of your disobedience, because of your rebelliousness.

83. And if you have caused affliction, then you will not live next to and beside the people. For then you will be persecuted, you will be driven away. That is how you will make rabbits, make deer of your wife, your children. Nowhere will your home stand, nowhere will you see its interior. From that place misery, that which troubles, that which torments people will come, emerge. Nowhere will you see your nopal, nowhere will you see your honey.[14] If thus you act, if thus you live, by your own accord you will demonstrate what sickens people, what troubles and torments them. By your own accord you will go among rags, among ruined wares. By your own accord you will accept what is vicious, what is wicked, what dishonors, what is bad, what is disobedience, headstrongness.[15]

---

12 Literally, "if you suddenly bite them."

13 Literally, "come here."

14 Meaning, effectively, "nowhere will you get sustenance."

15 *Tzonteyotl*, the term translated here as "headstrongness," is the vice of lacking humility.

84. It is sufficient for virtue[16] that when something is recommended to you, you listen calmly, and afterward, calmly, you will answer whether you will be able to do it, or whether it is not possible. You should not lie to people; you should only say what is right, only what is true, namely whether it is not possible or whether you will be able to do it. Reply not with reluctance, lest someone else receives the order. If you always act thus, you will be much loved. Not without care should you oversee the harvest, but you must place yourself well, pick things up well, plant them well, make them well rooted, sow them well in your fields, in your beds. Plant magueys, plant nopals. Make your house well so that there, with the help of and beside others, you may leave those you have educated, those you have supported, and those who have skirts and blouses. Tomorrow, or the day after tomorrow, the one who gives support, the one who gives help, will grow weary and weak.

85. The One by Whom We Live will safeguard, will protect you so that your face and your heart will be well, and well satisfied. Do not worry about, be not disturbed over what they will receive, because your heart knows well that you gave them all your protection when they came into the world, when they were born, when they lived on earth. And now, this is all that I thus bring to your hand, to your foot, to your chest, to your head, to your heart, to your body. Be strengthened, my son!

---

16 Literally, "it is already good, already right."

Response in which the son answers his father's word in this way (metaphorical language)

86. Your heart overflows[1] for me. On the earth sit, settle down,[2] my lord. Just now a lip, a mouth have come to spring, have come to fall. Your affliction, your weeping, your tears—by them I have become rich, by them I have become prosperous thanks to our Lord and to what is proper to you as mother, as father. May I adopt, may I receive your edification for men, your instruction for people.

87. What affects me? What do I think about? Is it only in the dung heap, only in the excrement pile that I find my home, my place to stand, my place to live, my place to go out?[3] Where there is a tail, a wing, some bricks, some mortar, I take it, I pick it up[4] because I am a common man, a farmer, a woodcutter, a peasant, because I was born poor. Because I have made him weep, I have saddened him, because from the front, from the side my Lord, the One by Whom We Live, has seen me. In this way I have listened to him, I have honored him.

88. Where He is, you have only to take, you have only to attend to what is proper to the mother, the father—which, perhaps, is not as the jade, the turquoise, as what fills your belly, your throat, as a coffer, a reed chest.[5] You have forgiven me, you have made me see if

---

1 More literally, "inclines toward me."

2 Literally, "let yourself fall."

3 The sentence means roughly "Am I one who lives in ignominy?"

4 Literally, "I take it for the people, I pick it up for the people."

5 In the Nahuatl, this sentence looks to have at least two transcription errors.

any place was risky, if it held dangers. In this way do your necklace, your quetzal plume, and your varied feathers shake,[6] thus do they unfold, do they spread, do they manifest themselves in an orderly way.

89. And because I am poor, because I am a common man, I shall only weep, I shall only suffer. I must not receive, I must not make your advice my own, if in some unclean place, if in the dung heap, I must throw, I must cast your weeping, your tears. For I have become rich, I have become prosperous thanks to the Lord and to you who have favored me. Sit on the earth, and give rest to your heart, to your body.

---

6 These are not a *difrasismo* for child, but for the father's edifying discourse, his words.

Exhortation in which our men speak to their women, whom they have married in church

90. My spouse, listen. May you take, may you accept what I will tell you only with much love. You will receive it happily, now that the Lord, who is divine and worthy of honor, who possesses prosperity and tranquility, the One by Whom We Live, favors us. His heart has thus made us captives, for it has bound us. Shall we only be silent? With all your breath,[1] with all your strength bind yourself to what is high. Be not discouraged. Stand beside Him and learn His stoop, His crookedness, the misery and destitution.[2] No longer does that ignorance cause you to be afflicted, to become ill. No longer for those reasons does your throat twist, and your bowels grow thin.[3]

91. Will heat shine down, will warmth fall on us alone? But this is how the Lord, our Lord *Dios*, consoles us, welcomes us with all His power. Throw, fling yourself down next to Him, for He Himself will become the root of our being. For thus is how it will be, thus is His word by which He reprimands us, by which He binds us; be mindful of Him everywhere. Go and draw near to your face, your heart. Go observing, go watching what it is that will be taken from you on earth. In the place where one seeks, where one paints,[4] little is that which goes,

---

1 The term in Nahuatl is the possessive form of *ihiyotl*, which is one of the three animating powers of the human person.

2 Meaning, "learn his lessons." I have followed Silva Galeana in this translation, but the statements appear to be missing a primary verb in Nahuatl.

3 Meaning, "for these reasons you are no longer discouraged."

4 Meaning, "on earth."

walks. Go realizing what will be misfortune, misery, what is only vanity, what is acting in front of and on top of people. You should not live thus. Only calmly, with prudence should you go to the front so that you do not inflame my chest.[5] May you live only with care, with calm. That is all, my beloved companion. Be grateful to our Lord Jesus Christ.

---

5 Meaning, "so that you do not shame me."

Response in which the woman returns the word to her husband

92. My dear child, my manly lord, I will hurt you, I will offend you, I will make you forget. You know much of the toil of servitude, the toil of tribute. Your dear heart overflows. Hence, I take, I make mine, I hear what you say to me. For the heart of the Lord, of our Lord, will be afflicted. Perhaps I will move him to compassion, or perhaps not, and perhaps that which must be followed, which must be straightened out, I will fulfill for you, so that by following it we may act rightly.

93. Will you be glad? Will you rejoice that your bowels have contracted?[1] Will you not weary them because we are commoners? For your net will only be a little spoiled;[2] you will go about suffering, my lad, my lord. I will trouble, I will disturb, will make you go nowhere, will not strengthen you, but rather He Who Lives, He Who Is, He Who Is Dear, He Who Is Desired will.[3] How will it be? Is it not true that I will make you ashamed, when before people I act not prudently? Will you make this the object of your anger? Should you not leave it in oblivion, when perhaps thus your heart, your body shall be loved, my lord, my lad.

---

1 Meaning, "Will you rejoice in suffering hardship?"

2 Meaning, "you will experience a bit of need."

3 I understand the series of unusual names to be used in the place of *Ipalnemohuani*, He by Whom We Live, or the One by Whom We Live.

94. For such is all that a lip, a mouth recounts, repays, returns, restores to your word as it is humbly manifest. On whom, perhaps, do you leave me? For I am become your flesh, your bones. Are you in truth hiding something from me, are you lying to me? For I will be what you guard, my manly lord. I express it to She Who Is Our Advocate, the righteously consecrated, divine maiden, who is always shining fully beside her beloved son, our Lord Jesus Christ.

Words of greeting by which some nobleman greets, speaks to one else who is a lord or noble

95. My lord, sit yourself down, perhaps for a moment, for a day, in the place of his sandals, on the left of the Lord of the Near and the Nigh, of the One Who Is the Home, the House—the only Lord, *Dios*, whom you serve as his sandal, on whose left you are, whom you assist, whom you help—you represent him, you are his image,[1] his eyes, his jaw. You have become his face, his ear because you serve as his interpreter—you make his voice, his words flow. The breath, the word of our Lord goes not in vain, falls not in vain, but rather is what goes blossoming, shining, ennobling, honoring. Next to you, in your hands He placed these. In your interior, in your entrails, your belly, your throat He hid, He put the book, the paints, that which is in red and black ink,[2] where the arrows of the eagle and ocelot appear—those that you are throwing, returning in that way.

96. And there is the great two-sided mirror, the one that appears, that you observe in the region of the dead, in the sky above. As it surveys in the place of the dead and the sky above, so you look at all the places of the earth. And there stands the thick torch, the one that does not smoke, the one that contains no mist, so that it dawns in all the regions of the world, so that its light, its radiance from your mount and

---

1 The term used in Nahuatl is a form of *ixiptla*, a philosophically loaded term that bears some relationship to questions surrounding personal identity.

2 This is a *difrasismo* for the written word and, by extension, wisdom.

water[3] may be observed. And He has given you hands and feet;[4] *Dios* has given you the tail and wing that are scattered, dispersed in your mount and water. You guide the city, you lead it, you make them love it. For this reason, our Lord has painted you, He has colored you,[5] He has given you lips and teeth,[6] dignity and honor. In this way He has strengthened you, clothed you, varnished you in white,[7] adorned you with feathers, has set you up, given you firmness.

97. You give honor to His government, to His lordship, you make Him prosper. In such a way you work hard for Him, intensely, you preside over His eagle mat, His ocelot mat. In this way he who is of high warrior rank lies—he who by day does not rest, does not lie down, lie flat. Next to him are his tooth and nail, his drinking and eating of people, the assent and descent—the snare for hunting, the rope, the trap hole, the obsidian, the stick and stone that thus destroy, that break the very jade and turquoise.[8]

98. And concerning the broad quetzal plume, the one that measures an arm, the undulating one, the very green one, the one that glistens well.[9] And the one who is very much an eagle and ocelot, who in his manner picks up, preserves, who bears new shoots, new blossoms, who blooms, who is renowned, receives honor, and in that way

---

3 This is a *difrasismo* for city.

4 Meaning, "He has given you subjects."

5 Meaning, "He has put wisdom in you."

6 Meaning, "He gave you the word to convince, and teeth to punish, to bite."

7 Meaning, "He comforted you."

8 The ruler appears here by way of a long list of attributes pertaining to his means of punishment, "tooth and nail," the "drinking and eating of people," etc.

9 This paragraph is devoted to an excellent man, metaphorically represented by a broad quetzal plume.

is tormented, suffers.[10] In that way he is slippery, slick before you and beside you. There where you are thus seated you shed tears, weeping. Your face, your heart, your body, your flesh suffer, are tormented. No longer peacefully, gently do you awake, do you arise. No longer do you sleep, do you rest peacefully, but rather you are startled; no longer with tranquility do you come to shine, to dawn[11] in how you will spend the day, the night.

99. And so we are only getting your sweat, your shadow.[12] Your face, your heart, are frightened, are carried away by water.[13] Your body dreads and you fear what may happen behind you. No longer goes there what you take, what you get, what you drink, what you eat— the precious water, *atole*, medicinal herb.[14] They only approach your lips, your mouth.[15] For these reasons is your heart in your hands.[16] Thus with difficulty, in the absence of tranquility do you exercise the lordly office, the government. In that way you help *Dios's* dear mount and water, his reed mat and seat.

100. And now, strengthen your heart, your body. Whom, in truth, will you leave in charge? Whom, in truth, do you observe? For you are already a mother, a father to the people. For you already edify, already instruct them. You are the one with the back,

---

10 The idea is that the man preserves the tradition and has children; they are new shoots and blossoms.

11 Meaning, "to be concerned with."

12 Meaning, "your protection."

13 Meaning, "you are afraid of not succeeding in your tasks."

14 Translating *tlapanquipahtli* by following Rémi Siméon's entry in his dictionary (1977).

15 Meaning, "you do not enjoy them."

16 Meaning, "you are worried."

you are the one with the burden. Great is what you carry, great is your responsibility, because you are the ceiba, ahuehuete, because you give shade, you give protection, because you are shelter and support. You are remedy and relief. Your subjects, those who are of your blood and color, those who are your shoots, your kin, your relatives, your kinsmen, your kindred move next to you, to your side. So too do your eyebrows, your nails, your beards,[17] those who are on your left, those who clad you with sandals,[18] your mothers, your fathers. Finally, those who are dispersed and scattered, those who are your tail and wing,[19] those who are your hands, your feet, all those who under your shade, under your protection enter.

101.   In this way, you become like various fruit trees, meaning you grow by what is sweet and pleasant. Various birds—the hummingbird, the *zaquan*, the *quecholli*, the *tzinitzcan*, the quetzal—flutter about you.[20] In your hands they shelter from the heat, they protect themselves from the sun. And so, in your hands is placed the jade

---

17 These were thought of as extensions of the human body, so that the sense is that these are "your grandchildren, your descendants."

18 Meaning, "those who serve you."

19 "Those who are dispersed and scattered" are "the people," while "your tail and wing" means "your subjects."

20 The text literally reads that these birds "suck" from you—suggesting that they derive sustenance this way. Following Silva Galeana's historical notes, each bird might be described as follows: The *zaquan* is a bird with bright yellow plumage, about the size of a canary. The *quecholli* is a brilliant bird that has been called the flamingo by some. The *tzinitzcan* is a bird with shiny black plumage, about the size of pigeon, that was used as an ornament in various works. The quetzal is a green-feathered bird, very beautiful and highly appreciated; it is their tail feathers that were called *quetzalli*, which the present text translates as "quetzal plume."

vessel. There too are the yellow and blue waters in which the people,[21] covered with dew, stand so that you can shake the waters over them. In that way you wash, you bathe the people. And in your hands lies the thick broom, the wide comb with which you groom, with which you comb the people. And in your hands lies the scorpion, the nettle, the cold water, and the thin stick[22] by which you strike people. In that way you edify, you instruct them. And in your hands lie the reed, the fine sand, the coarse rush with which you scrape, with which you thin, with which you polish.

102. And you choose, you make the jade equal to the thin, the well-formed, the well-pierced, the well-rounded one, equal to the wide turquoise, the well-roughened one, to the well-thinned jade, the perfect, the one that shines.[23] You have unfolded, you have put in order the necklaces and quetzal plumes, those of good beginning, those of good ending, those that measure well an arm, the undulating ones, the very green ones, the ones that glitter. And you choose, you put in order the valued items, the varied and fine feathers—those of the *xiuh*,[24] the *tlauhquechol*,[25] the *tzinitzcan*, the *zaquan*. You take care of, you guard them. In their own spot you place them, in their own shelter you put them, where they are you spread them out. Because you paint, you color, the books, what is written, because you put forth the red and black ink,

---

21 Literally, "reeds."

22 These are metaphors for instruments of punishment.

23 Meaning, "you make the good word (or teaching) equal to the best."

24 A bird with green plumage, also called the *elotototl*.

25 A red-headed and red-necked bird, which inhabits mainly the Totonacapan region.

the model, the measure, the example, the paragon, the pattern.[26] As you work the stick and stone, so you draw yourself. You will never be forgotten, your fame, your renown will never be lost.

103. And in your hands is the great mirror, the great torch by whose light you come to look over the mount and water, by which you come to be mentioned, honored. In this way you lead, you carry the load, you guide, you fortify them on the path, because you have become a mother, a father. The owner of the earth, *Dios*, has favored you. Give Him honor, exalt His quality as a mother, as a father, His charge, His lordship, His leadership, His fame, His honor. In that way take heart, gird yourself, fortify yourself, be strong. In that way weep, be sad, be enlivened, observe well because it is difficult, because it is heavy what our Lord has set up for you. Fall not into decadence,[27] nor lag behind, nor harm your back,[28] nor lose command. Cast yourself not into the water, the straits.[29] Do not faint, nor lose heart.

104. And also do not go up against others, nor hurl yourself against the people in their governance, in their place of command from *Dios*—He Who also has given you very little time, Who still one day has come to guard His mount and water. A long time ago the lords, the rulers acted to lay the foundation, to establish the principle

---

26 This statement is a composition of several longer three-term metaphors, rather than the two-term *difrasismos*, and can be understood as meaning "you are the one who promotes knowledge and the one who sets the example."

27 Literally, "do not cause yourself to leave behind your *ihiyotl*," which may be translated a little less literally as "do nothing to cause your exhaustion." *Ihiyotl* is one of the central animating forces of the body associated directly with breath.

28 The back is here used, metaphorically, as that by which a leader carries his people, just as a worker carries a load.

29 Meaning, "do not expose yourself to danger or put yourself in a precarious place."

of the command, of the government. They no longer come to see, they no longer come to learn what comes after them, what is later; they will no longer come to pass by, they will no longer come to stand tomorrow, the day after tomorrow; they will no longer come to give strength to your heart, to your body; and they will no longer come to give you a lip, a mouth, nor the weeping, the tears so that you may be strengthened, invigorated, you, my necklace, my quetzal plume.[30]

105. For that is why they began to cry, why they began to suffer, why they began to weep, to shed their tears on the reed mat and seat. They knew not only of joys; everywhere their face, their heart was wasting away. Thus they came to lead, they came to bear the load; they did not neglect their mount and water, their reed mat and seat. For those alone He suffered, His heart was afflicted in the day, in the night. With difficulty, without any tranquility, they went to attempt their sleep, their rest. The model, the example, the pattern, the paragon, the measure, the red and black ink, the books, what is written—they drew them, they painted them. Their fame, their glory, their name, their history are never forgotten, never lost. As stone and wood are worked, so they were carved, they left their painted trace—they left the light, the torch, the mirror.[31]

106. Everywhere they burnished, they polished, they added value, they put order; peacefully, gently, calmly they arranged the things in the coffer, the reed chest. It is great the shade, the shelter that they went to make, to found—the thick ceiba, the ahuehuete that stand with saplings and leaves, that they did not neglect, nor oppress

---

30 Meaning, in this case, "my respectable, my honorable sir."

31 "Mirror" in this case means "a good example."

anything in favor of sleeping. They do not go yanking lips.[32] Peacefully, gently, calmly, on their legs, in their arms, on their backs, they went to put the one who wanders aimlessly, the one who crawls, the one who plays with earth, the one who plays with pot shards, the one who stays in the net, in the tree.

107. And the old man, the old woman, together with the destitute, the wretched, the discontented, the unhappy, the joyless, the one in whom his bowels are attached,[33] there where emerges what makes one hurt, what makes one suffer, what causes pain. Not seen are his sustenance and livelihood, and he remains in misery. They are those who go shedding tears, who go biting their fingernails, go tie their hands. Where the wild beasts are, among the stone fences, in the corners, the bereaved, the wretched go suffering. In the grasslands, in the forests, the chili, the salt, the edible herbs, the cactus, the firewood, the water that they seek, that they collect, tire them out. And they stir anxiety in the market, in the plaza; they go about tormented, they go about suffering, their hearts, their bodies, their lips are parched. There the bereaved, the wretched go forth; there what is spicy, what afflicts goes forth; nearby there go forth what sickens, what frightens; the Lord of the Near and the Nigh takes care of that.

108. Perhaps also the lords, the leaders have left upon you the guidance, the channeling, that which educates humans, that which instructs them. Place next to you those who are your feet, your hands. And be not lazy in embracing your duty, nor be lazy in carrying your burden. Do not neglect, nor leave behind your mount and water, but benefit them. I will not make you contract the illness, nor

---

32 Meaning, "forcing others to speak."

33 Meaning, "he who is in misery."

make you receive punishment, nor have you cover yourself with shadow because you work hard, intensely. For the tasks of command, of ruler-ship that you carry are many. In that way you lead, you bear the burdens of your mount and water. This is all. A lip, a mouth thus I bring near to your hands, to your feet, to your chest, to your head. Be strengthened, my lord!

Answer in which the ruler replies to the gentleman who greeted him

109. My younger brother, you have toiled, settle down on the earth.[1] Your heart has been generous, you have done justice to the reed mat and seat of our Lord, *Dios*. I must deem myself worthy, I must deem that I deserve a lip, a mouth that has come to go forth, that has come to fall from your belly, from your throat, that which you have scattered, that which you have disseminated is real jade, genuine turquoise; it is the well-rounded, the well-formed, the well-smoothed, the well-buffed, the finely thinned, the well-pierced, the perfected, the resplendent, the translucent. Moreover, the broad quetzal plume, the one that well measures an arm, the one that undulates, the one that has yet its base, has yet its tip, that one, I mean, I put not just anywhere, but rather I place it on its mat. I nowhere throw, spill the lordship, the government, on a dung heap, on an excrement heap, nor do I throw away your weeping, your tears, by which you comfort me, console, and exalt me.

110. I must not laugh at your words; I must not take them as a joke. If I had wept, if I had grieved, if I had shown modesty, if I had been grateful, if I had been edified, I would have taken them, I would have made them mine. I would have introduced them to my belly, to my throat; I would have brought them close to me. Where your people are, only there take and attend to the leadership,[2] to the government, to the proprietors, to he who carries others, which is characteris-

---

1 Literally, "let yourself fall on the ground."

2 Literally, "lordship."

tic of mothers, fathers, as our Lord wishes. For you have paid, you have made restitution with something that is before Him, before His mount and water, before His reed mat and seat.[3] And now, that is all. With a lip, with a mouth I return your breath, your word. You have done right by me, and your heart has been pained. Give your body rest, settle down on the ground,[4] my little brother.

---

3 Meaning, "in his presence and before his place of command."
4 Literally, "let yourself fall on the ground."

Salutations by which a lady greets, speaks
to another who is also a lady

111. My dear child, my dear lady, be strengthened. Perhaps for a short time here, for a day, you slave away, you work beside our Lord, the One by Whom We Live, *Dios*. You sweep, you clean for him. For a short time, for a day, you wake up hastily from sleep, you learn by dreams thanks to Him, the Lord of the Home, the House, the One who has the strength to embrace, to carry on his back. Perhaps your weeping, your tears, your sighs, your affliction transpire because you make our Lord, the Lord of the Near and the Nigh sigh and grieve.

112. You, my lady, feel the weight of your obligations. Give strength to your heart, to your body, concerning the Only God, the One by Whom We Live. You who are a poor girl, falter not, but serve Him with all your strength, straining your dear heart. Whom, in truth, have you scouted? To whom, in truth, do you leave (1) the mount and water, the reed mat and seat, (2) the lords, those who command, the young, the children, (3) the mothers, the fathers, the tail and wing, (4) the destitute, the wretched, the one who weeps, the one who eats his nails, the one who with difficulty, painfully, earns his living?[1]

113. For all are the subjects of your care, of your guidance, whom our Lord entrusted to you, gave you to safe-keep, so that you might edify and educate them. You are like a *zaquan* bird, like a

---

1 In Nahuatl the sequence of grouped terms is denoted by the use of *auh*, which is here rendered by numerals in parentheses.

quetzal. Long are your wings and tail,[2] which the Lord has given you. In this way you edify and guide people. In this way, near and nigh to you, your children, whom you educate, will come to gather round, so that you may relieve, so that you may give remedy to their hearts, to their bodies. Not one, not two are you to abandon, to leave behind because your supporting embrace, your burdened back, are great, because your waist equipment and your shoulder gear are great,[3] because you are relief and remedy, because what is sweet and pleasant comes from your hand.

114. Peacefully, gently, place in them, in their mouths, a little of your effort, your vigor, cup of cocoa, the folded tortillas— make them desire it.[4] Not the filth and dust are you to make them drink or eat, so that you do not provoke sickness for those you edify and educate. Rather, peacefully, gently, educate and edify them. Do not wish to make them equal, nor disturb their sleep; do not stoop down or lower yourself, but rather bring close to you those who are your hands, your feet,[5] those who are your burden, those whom you carry on your shoulders. May you be able to extend, may you be able to broaden your burden, your responsibility.

115. And strengthen your tail and wing. Carry them close to you, spread your arms for them. Straighten them out so that they have shade near, nigh to you, so that your children are protected from the heat. In that way, their face, their heart, their body, their flesh will not be afflicted, they will not suffer; in that way they will spread

---

2 Meaning, "your political office and station is a precious charge."

3 These are *difrasismos* for the responsibilities associated with governing.

4 Meaning, "habituate them in that which profits and strengthens."

5 Meaning, "give protection to those who are your subjects."

out, they will flutter[6] close to you because nothing will afflict them. In that way, with peace, they will be edified, they will be strengthened so that their faces, their hearts will also fare[7] well, thanks to the mount and water. In the same way, your reed mat, your seat will be greatly exalted; in the same way, they will lower their heads before you, they will bow humbly, they will show you recognition, gratitude, to you who are their mother, their father, their protector.

116. In this way you will also be worthy of the mount and water's weeping, their tears. What remains of the flower, remains of the tobacco, the aroma, the cup of cocoa, the folded tortilla is there. And by acting in this way you will be able to take and receive them. In this way you will drink them, you will eat them where you educate, where you instruct. Thus, you will not be ashamed, but exalted before the people, so that a lip, a mouth, your breath, your word—whatever you want your children to do, because you educate and edify them—may emerge, may fall well. And from the eagles, the ocelots, you will well deserve their elbow, their knee, their shoulder, their back,[8] where one hoe, where two hoes are necessary. So will they help in your planting beds where there is need of some adobe, a blob of clay—or where there is need of some snaring rods, or in some place where sweeping, where cleaning is to be done.

117. And for those who have a skirt and blouse, you will also be able to deserve what comes into their hands, what comes out of their hands—perhaps only a spindle, two spindles, or the water

---

6 The metaphorical suggestion is that the village is considered here as a group of birds.

7 Literally, "go" in Nahuatl.

8 Meaning, "they will dedicate their whole body to work for you."

and metate.[9] They will help you and in that way they will also fare well. And perhaps sometime they will seek a mother, a father,[10] and before you they will place their weeping, their tears, their destitution, their wretched state.[11] Somewhere too they will place a little bit of what they have set aside, of what they have sought, their elbow, their knee,[12] their sweetness, their savor, the chili, the salt, the edible herb, what is taken from the nopal, what is given to the people to drink, what is given to them to eat. Together with that they will place what is earned with the spindle, with the weaving board, by those who have skirts, those who have blouses, or they will be weeping, be tearful. On your lips, in your mouth, they will put the *atole*, the folded tortilla, the vegetable, the nopal. Perhaps they will also peacefully, gently pick these up for you, they will take them to you—you who are their mother, you who are their shelter—because you love them, you help them, you are their guide, you are their mistress.

118. And so, when the Lord, our Lord, the Lord of the earth, the One by Whom We Live, gets tired, He will take you, He will hide you. Then they will weep for you, they will grieve, they will be distressed, they will remember your love for the people, your help, your benevolence, your indulgence, because you never abandoned them with disdain, because you never left them behind, because you never sheltered them lazily but protected them, because you did not live in front of them, on top of them, because you did not go on to do damage to your

---

9 Meaning, "you will deserve the fruits of your women's labor."

10 Meaning, "protection."

11 Both terms used here for destitution and wretchedness turn on forms of *icnot-lacayotl*, which is also the state of being an orphan.

12 Meaning, "effort."

reed mat and seat, your mount.[13] For you should not throw mud on the people, nor should you hate them, for you should not go crumbling, nor should you go scattering, you should not disgrace yourself, nor should you debase yourself. Only peacefully, only gently should you give place to your mount and water, to your reed mat and seat.

119. Only thus should it be: as is customary, as things usually are, as they are arranged, so you should leave them. As a result, nothing will be reproached to you, nothing will be murmured against you. Only peacefully, only gently, do you endure hunger, do you suffer scarcity, do you submit in the land of our Lord.

My lass, my lady, if you so perform your management—the carrying on your shoulders, what is proper to a mother, a father—well, then you will go on to enjoy great renown and reputation. Your fame, your glory will never be forgotten, never be lost; as stone and wood are carved and painted, so you will leave a picture of yourself on earth.

120. For if you do not weep, if you do not mourn for what our Lord gave you as a gift, as what you deserve, what is managed, what is carried on your shoulders, together with all His gifts that He placed in you to give you fame, to exalt you, only by what is proper to you, by your own actions will you leave them on earth. For only by your own actions will you throw yourself into the water, fall into the precipice, throw yourself into the coals, into the fire.

121. And if you do not act thus, if instead you wept for Him, if you moved our Lord to compassion, if you take part in His guidance, His burden, and all that He wills, then you will rejoice, you

---

13 This appears to be half the typical *difrasismo* "mount and water," meaning "city" or "people."

will be proud. Thanks be to Him. For those reasons you will go to Him, go up to His house in heaven—there He will come to receive you.

And I will not make what is bad[14] overtake you, cover you in shadow. Because you work hard, you work with intensity, I will make you forget about it, erase it. With a lip, a mouth—like this I come near to your hands, your feet, your chest, your head. Be strengthened, my dear girl.

---

14 Literally the combination of *temoxtli* and *ehecatl* means "pestilence," but a metaphorical sense looks to be at work here.

Answer given by the lady who has been visited

122. Your heart, my daughter, has bestowed a bounty upon me; you have given me a just reward. Thanks to our Lord I have enjoyed myself, I have taken solace; and thanks to His mount and water, to His reed mat and seat, and also thanks to the lords of the mount and water here I have heard the weeping, the sobbing. What is the matter with me, what do I consider myself? Because I am a spoiled skirt, a ragged blouse,[1] I shall not cast in the dunghill, throw into the refuse your cries and your tears. In that way you invigorate me, you exalt me. I will only weep, I will only be moved by your quality as a mother, a father. You have done right by me. Be strengthened, my older sister.

---

1 Meaning, "I am a modest and insignificant person."

Words of exhortation from nobles, rulers of Tetzcoco, who spoke in this manner to the neighbors there, long ago, and with this discourse make them see how the Lord Jesus Christ came here

123. Here you are, you who are tail, you who are wing, understand this turquoise, this jade.[1] You are of the people, you are a neighbor. Why do you not pick up, do you not make your own what comes from our Lord's representative, His interpreter, His glory, His fame? He has opened his coffer, his reed chest to you; he already crumbles, scatters what is linked to your mother, your father, the *padre*, the great ceiba, the great ahuehuete, their canopy,[2] beneath which you find yourself shade and protect yourself from the sun. Give the people a mother, a father;[3] you who are a poor eagle, a poor ocelot.

124. You are a son in need. Grieve, languish no more. In places like the grasslands, in the woods, you weep, you anguish, you seek your day's sustenance and your descent or ascent.[4] And you who are a skirt and blouse, when you place yourself where the people's thread, where the people's weaving board is,[5] there you edify and educate the one who plays with earth, the one who gathers pot shards, the one

---

1 Meaning, "you who are subjects, accept and understand this precious admonition."

2 Reading *malacayoticac* for *malacoyoticac*.

3 Meaning, "give them protection."

4 Meaning, "your fortune or misfortune."

5 Meaning, "when you act to help people doing the work appropriate to a woman's role."

who rejoices with stones, the one who rejoices with wood. You will take
on the well-polished jade, the well-worked precious metal, the broad and
very green quetzal feather from those who show you something, from
what they put inside you, what they bind in you, what they place in your
throat.

125. Where there is mount and water, you afflict the scepter,
the carrying frame, you lower them to the ravine, you
climb the hill;[6] you shed your tears, you feel fatigue. And where you have
gone to find a vast land, amid your sweat you have received it in your
hands. You are a poor man, you have gone between the stone fences,
you sit next to the walls,[7] where your nails rot. Perhaps somewhere you
will come to be admonished. You take pains for a bit of chili, for a gran-
ule of salt to strengthen yourself, to grow firm. The breath of the Lord,
Dios who made us, if you do not truly accept it, if you do not make it
your own, then when it tires, when the one who carries and bears us, is
annoyed, it will come down on you. Our Lord should enter your interior.

126. Do you feel stonelike, strong? Do you want to become a
stick, a stone? Perhaps you will place yourself in a hollow
stone? Perhaps you will go in the water, the mount, the cave? Has our
Lord become tired, has He become angry, has He become disdainful,
does He only cause dissatisfaction? We are like that, we are subjects, we
are mud. He will rule us in the way He understands. Take charge of your
descent or ascent wherever you go; you are a woodcutter, a husbandman,
a digging stick, a tool to carry. And you are a spindle, a weaving board;[8]

---

6 Meaning, "in your activities, you are busy."

7 Meaning, "you live in destitution."

8 The phrases "[to be] a digging stick, a tool to carry" and "spindle, weaving board,"
mean to know how to carry out the activities proper to the roles of men and women.

you are someone's hair, someone's nails.[9] In this case you will strive in this way, where mortar is mixed.

127. In *Dios's* lap, in His shelter, you will go to be—where His guiding rod, His canopy is—go to place yourself at his side. He will say when He has felt annoyance; He will place you at his feet. We are not stony, nor are we hard. Look above, to what surpasses us, in the interior of heaven; there is the wealth of our Lord, of the beloved son, Jesus Christ, the true man, the friend, the beloved, the one who bestows, who determines, who brings things down. And you are the subject, you are what is carried on His back; listen well to Him, keep Him in your heart. Forget not that which is to be kept, what He gives you, what God makes you drink, what I put in you. Take in your hand what God places in you, namely what goes, what gives profit.

128. And if you do not receive it well, He will show you His place there used for throwing, for hurling people, His place of torment. There they find the dust and filth, the stick and stone. There they are setting their unkempt, filthy throne. God will have thrown you next to them; He will have punished you against them. Then, and there, in your torment, in your affliction, you will say: "For it is true what my mother, my father said, I should have received, I should have made their word mine. It has happened, how wretched I am!" And already now, I urge you to receive it, what your mothers, your fathers did not see. Now thus be happy, rejoice.

129. And turn behind you, behind your back, and tell your heart that you did not know what is now going to be given to you, that the coffer, the reed chest is now open to you; watch it attentively, give yourself entirely to our Lord, *Dios*. Perhaps you took, you

---

9 Meaning, "you are an outgrowth of your parent."

received a lip, a mouth. His breath, His word, keep them in your heart, may they not make you dizzy, may they not intoxicate you; be not so proud that our Lord, *Dios*, will be angry, show disdain. And His fame, His honor, by which alone there[10] one is made happy, there He will give it to the people, He will inspire, He will infuse it into them.

130. Just look attentively at your Lord, Who acts like a good bird. At His tails, His wings[11] are placed our mother, our father, who govern those of us who are in all parts of the world. You will see that at present our Lord Jesus Christ abandons nothing and no one. He will pour his jade, his blue waters with his jade vessel. So He will wash, He will cleanse your soul,[12] your life. In that way they will be cleansed so that you will live well at His side; one moment, one day you will ask for them as a loan from our Lord. Place yourself at His side, go with attention to your God, your Lord, your Master. He will be grieved; He will be angry when you cause Him displeasure; He will return it to your heart; He will make it one.

131. Still enjoy wealth from Him who sets you straight, from Him who makes you clean. And since in this way He will make a subject clean, you will go and place yourself into the hands of our Lord Jesus Christ. And now that He will be kind to you, weep deep within you, grieve deep within you; do not disdain him, do not make something dance within you, do not be covetous, do not say, "Does He indeed make you clean, straight?"[13] Do not be like that, but only earn

---

10 Meaning, "in heaven."

11 Meaning, "the common folk."

12 The term used here for "soul" is the *yolia*. This was but one energizing force of the body for precontact Nahuas.

13 Meaning, "don't be distrusting." Also, one notes that the Christian interpola-

kindness before our Lord. Go bow your head down and kneel, go bow down with reverence, go accustoming your feet. It is slippery, slick before God; if with something slippery you thus fall, you trip, your life will receive honor, will be firm. Go on only bowing down, go on earning benevolence; peacefully our Lord, the divine man, Jesus Christ, will receive you. And now, perhaps He will be kind to you, He, our Lord, will lay His blessed hand upon you.

132. And now, perhaps in this way you will make yourself clean, perhaps in this way you will live well on earth. Now do you draw near to His riches, which come with Him, or will you once more offend Him? Will you thus blacken, stain your soul, your *anima*?[14] And so, when you remember our Lord, once again you will make yourself clean before Him, you will lay before Him that which covers you with black, your stain;[15] and then, once again, He will have compassion on you, He will see you with benevolence.

God, the Lord, He knows, He produces what you require; he who obeys the precepts of God straightens well, gives cleanliness to his soul, to his *anima*. He gives it to him so that he may live well, so that he may go satisfied before our Lord, so that the moment, that one day, he might invoke Him, implore Him, that the perverse beings may not approach Him.

133. Now also enjoy, also partake of His richness, that which with our Lord comes, because He has made it clean, He has made it straight for us; because we have heard, we have known His

---

tion here uses cleanliness and straightness rather than goodness and straightness, the pre-invasion Nahua terms for virtue.

14 The term in *Nahuatl* is a hybridism, *manima*.

15 The suggestion is that you should confess.

breath, His straight, clean word, which He shows, places before us. Our Father, the *Padre*, does not want all that others say, what they express, but only what He ordered through our Lord Jesus Christ. In that way He indicated the teaching to those whom He entrusted that everywhere we are taught to announce His blessed water[16] in the world to straighten people, to give them cleanliness, to bestow on people the benevolence, goodness of our Lord.[17]

134. Listen you who are subjects, thus He gives cleanliness to the people, keep Him well in your hearts, observe Him attentively, in this way correct yourselves, in this way observe the teaching of our Lord, for this is how we shall live well on earth. In this way we will invoke Him, we will implore Him, and we will remember our mother Holy Mary so that she may pray to Him for us, so that she may appease the heart of her beloved Son, our Lord Jesus Christ, so that He may give us life. And now, that is all.

---

16 There was also a pre-invasion form of a Nahua "baptism."

17 The phrase *in teoyotica iatzin*, "the blessed water," is one expression adopted to mean "baptism."

Here is how the rulers converse about government, so that the mount and water may not be ruined in their hands, that they may carry it well on their shoulders, that they may have it in their charge, that they may lead the tail and wing well. In this exhortation other peoples may take example.

135. My children, here you are, and here I stand, a poor old man. I am your mother, your father. My heart desires that you live peacefully, gently; receive what I tell you, what is thus understood, what is thus grasped, what is thus profitable. The lordship, the bond of birth, is said to be enjoyed by those who have access. Be not thereby presumptuous, be not puffed up, for you are of noble lineage. Behold, how you will seem so, how you will be mentioned, how you will be recognized as a result. It is quite necessary that you lower your heads, that you bow yourselves with humility, that you have affection for one another; and that you attend to the people's cloak, breechcloth, lip plug, and ear plug.

136. Nowhere ought you live in front of and on top of the people. Peacefully, calmly go about your lives. Have much respect for the poor old men, old women. And for the eagle, the ocelot, the commoner, have reverence;[1] look with respect on his tattered breechcloth, his ragged cloak. Wherever you meet the poor old man, by the river, on the road, you will say to him: "My father, my grandfather, my

---

1 The term used for "reverence" here also means "to fear, to have awe for." It is translated variously in the passages that follow.

uncle."[2] And to the old woman you will say: "My mother, my grand-mother, peacefully, calmly, go on your way, lest you fall somewhere."

137.

You should speak to them in such a way, for then they should show gratitude. In that way they will recognize in you one of lineage, one who is not inebriated, who is not proud of nobility, of the bond of descent. In that way will they fear you, will they look upon you with respect. And it would not be right that you make jokes or mock the man who is unfortunate, the blind, the deaf, the maimed, the crippled, the dirty. It is necessary that you have reverence for all people, that you look at them with humility, that you respect them. And, my son, if you only despise them, then of your accord, by your whim, you will hate yourself. It will not be true that you despise them. For otherwise, you will abandon the lineage, the bond of descent; in that case you will deserve the ragged breechcloth, the tattered cloak.

---

2 A greeting that treats another as an elder relative was taken to be a sign of respect.

Here is the exhortation to the already prudent, to the already grown-up youngster

138. My children, you are here, have reverence for another's wife, another's husband. Do not commit adultery,[1] do not get drunk, do not indulge in ball games, in the game of fortune. Speak not of your lineage, of your condition as men. Behold what makes a nobleman, what makes a man of lineage, now watch well: take good care of what you thus receive, of what you thus get, namely the digging and sod-breaking sticks.[2] Now take, receive the torch, the soap, the chili, the lime, the very thing that makes men of lineage, that which makes them lords.

139. With tears and worry one takes, one receives lordship, nobility. Already warm, already heated is the reed mat, the seat, that which concerns the home and house. In that way our wife, our daughter, will be happy. Let it not be said that we have not made use of, that we have taken our life in vain; with our hand, with our foot, with our face, with our heart, with our lives well led we will be given the lordship and nobility that we now so deserve, that thanks to the people we drink, we eat. And now we say that we will make use of it, that you will do so moderately. In that way you will become one of lineage, in that way you will become noble.

---

1 The term at stake, a form of *tetlaxincayotl*, derives from *xima*, meaning "to shave." While the Christian term "adultery" thus turns on adding an impurity of some sort to a relationship, the Nahua conception turns on shaving or sheering away what keeps a marriage, literally a "meet or joining" (*inamic*), together. Effectively, the metaphorical notion behind the admonition is "don't split up what is joined."

2 Metaphorically meaning, "the commoners," those who work with these instruments.

Here is the exhortation to the gentlemen, the aldermen, and the mayors,[1] who have been elected in this way

140. You have come to the lordship, you have approached the nobility; be afraid of them, lest they make you drunk, lest they make you proud. Respond moderately because it is a place for the mount and water. Certainly, you will do your task peacefully, settle moderately.[2] Peacefully, gently respond to the lord, to the noble; with the word of the mount and water[3] is how so you will take the land and mount well,[4] it is how you will carry out the lordship and nobility. In no place cause disputes among the lords, among those of lineage; do not ruin the reed mat, the seat. And peacefully talk about the one who rises, the one who crawls,[5] and the eagle, the ocelot.

---

1 "*Alcaldes, regidores*" is in Spanish in the original text.

2 Throughout this paragraph, the term *ihuiyan* means, by turns, "moderately" or "peacefully." The speaker is playing on the distinct but related valences of the word.

3 Meaning, "the people of the city."

4 This should be understood as "you will take charge of the people."

5 Meaning, "the children."

Here is what relieves, what heals people. When someone who has harmed something important of a gentleman, of one of lineage, when that someone has committed adultery, has stolen.

141. Congratulate yourself, my son, my lord, who exercise command. Behold, I have come to lay my fault before you, the filth that is in me; I have stolen, I have committed adultery, I have lived in front of and on top of people. You will relieve me; you will heal me. Say I will just fall into the ravine, into the precipice; say I will just be thrown, I will only be beaten by the hail, by the wind. There will only be relief, there will be healing now that I make you my mother, my father. I have come to take relief with you, with you I have come to be healed. On whom shall I hang myself?[1] You have become like a reed, like a willow,[2] that is why I have come to hold you, I have come to embrace you. You are a ceiba, you are an ahuehuete; you are relief and remedy; in your hands I will become green, I will grow new shoots; I will become clean, you will wash me, you will bathe me. Here is my resting place, my place of healing. Peacefully, gently your great-grandparents, your grandparents, the mat, the seat, the place where you are, gave relief to the people.

---

1 Meaning, "to whom shall I entrust myself?"
2 Meaning, "you can offer me protection."

Here is the admonition of other elders who, in Tepeyacac, were instructing in this way

142. Attend[1] my disciples, those whom I educate, to what I will tell you, to what is your formation, your observation, to the breath, to the wonderful word of *Dios*, to His opening of eyes, opening of ears, to His mirror. Receive well and make yours what are your gift, your desert, and your obligations because you are *Dios's* human workmanship; you are the tail and wing; you are turquoise, necklace, quetzal plume; you are generous, you are the abundance of small ears of corn. And you are the reed mat and seat, you have been honored, you have been elevated in dignity by the one God, *Dios*. Receive well that which I tell you, that which I warn you so that you may live correctly, so that you may follow the path with righteousness on *Dios's* earth, so that you may be the model of those who will still bloom, of those who will still sprout, of those who will go behind you, of those who will follow you so that you may give them good example, good principles.

143. Moreover, now I fit you with sandals,[2] on your left side I place the advice, the warning of the people, the eagle and ocelot, the skirt and blouse, their abundance of barbs and thorns from the mount and water.[3] Make your life well from this, which already *Dios* makes pleasant for you, already spreads its savor, its sweetness, its word.

---

1 Literally, "listen," although the term broadly means to understand by way of listening. This more neutral translation fits better with the activities that follow.

2 Meaning, "I am the one who does you a service."

3 Meaning, "the many children and neighbors of the town."

May that which is received, that which is taken, that which gives life, that which stands you on your feet in the world enter well in your ears, and come down, so that you may firmly leave your aromatic flowers,[4] your mushrooms, your medicinal plant, your blindness, your stupefying herbs, your gloom, your blackness, the stain with which you lived a long time ago.

144. And now, behold the breath, the word of the Lord of the Near and the Nigh, which I relate to you, which I lift up to your ears, of how the true God, *Dios*, is only one. I do not hide it from you, I do not conceal it from you, I do not incur falsehood in manifesting what He desires; because we, the interpreters of God, declare to you what was introduced in our belly, in our breast.[5] That is why we have come to cleanse, to give cleanliness to your *anima* so that it may cast out the filth and dust that it has, cast out its stench, its rottenness, which those who have the blackness and filth, namely, the *tzitzimime*,[6] the owl-men, put in it.

145. And with that we are done because we are mothers, we are fathers with respect to the divine things of the mount and water;[7] thus, in our lap, on our back you who are His tail and wing, follow the path of our Lord, you whom we educate, instruct in that which concerns the divine. In this way we lay down, we raise God's children; thus we make them spend the day, the night, because our quality as mothers, as fathers, our leading, our carrying on our shoulders has already shone forth. Because not within us, not in our entrails do we hide the mercies

---

4 Indicating hallucinogenic herbs.

5 Literally, "belly, throat."

6 These were thought to be an evil deity that inhabits the air.

7 Meaning, "with respect to those who live in the city."

that He does, namely how the One by Whom We Live exalts people in His house, in heaven. We do not whisper it, we do not murmur it, we express it to you, we explain it to you, we do not hide it from you, we do not deceive you, because we only want you to be comforted, to bind your waist so that you may be strengthened, because with it, with a modest life, you will be redeemed.

146. And always keep, put in your belly, your throat, what those who teach you, who instruct you, the Fathers,[8] tell you. And what do you do about it? Do you suffer hardships, are you needy? Are you an uncultured man[9] of uncertain origin? What makes you drunk? What makes you pant? What makes you jump? What makes you doubt? Do you still want to follow your path, your principles, those that your grandparents followed? The liars, the owlmen are only an object of scorn, mockery for the others; they are only blindness, they only lead people, they only bring them down to the place where they throw people, in their prison, in the place of mockery—that of the One by Whom We Live, *Dios*.

147. And this is where you ardently desire something, where you are sent. Will you only conjecture that perhaps there in the Land of the Dead, or perhaps there in heaven? But we have told you, we have suggested to you how we are to execute, to complete the

---

8 In Nahuatl, the term is the Spanish-Nahuatl *Padreme*. All such capitalized appearances in English refer to this term.

9 The Nahuatl is unclear at this point as the present interpretation does not make grammatical sense. The literal phrase asks, "do you have *tami* clothing?" The *Tamime* were a people of the itinerant Chichimeca family. The translation uses a paraphrase for this family of ideas. David Bowles, in correspondence, has identified other uses of the term, but agrees that it sits poorly in the present context. There is something of a scholarly mystery here.

divine precepts. When God determines it, already there, at your end, where you are placed, at the moment of your death, you will not feel displeasure, you will not be distressed, you will not declaim your mothers, your fathers, the Fathers, because near to, next to you they will not have brought,[10] they will not have made the scorpion and nettle—such torment, affliction from the people of Our Lord—come close.

148. And when *Dios* so disposes, then He will cast you into the hands of the great owlman of the region of the dead, God's prison steward in the Land of the Dead, if you take not well that which comes from Him. And do you desire this already, do you long for it much? For we have already told you what is required, to dwell in another place. And listen well, not like a stranger are you to become acquainted with God's gift, but receive, make your own its quality as a mother, a father, its shelter, its protection, its edifying, its educating of people by those to whom God entrusted the teaching, the Fathers.

149. You are wretched, unhappy, you are discontented, afflicted; speak humbly to Him, humbly entreat the Lord of Riches, from whom is our flesh, the One by Whom We Live, the God of heaven, to grant your dinner and breakfast. In this way you will be exalted and grow. In this way will you receive warmth and be warmed. In the meantime, you suffer the edible roots, the herbal water, the mead, the roasted corn, the medicinal herb by which you rise, by which you lie down.

150. With the sprouts, the nopal making you strong,[11] follow the path on our Lord's earth. Call upon Him, for He

---

10 The sentence in Nahuatl uses all future-tense constructions, but I have changed the verbs' modality to make this and related constructions in these passages readable in English. Additionally, I have added the "not" for the sake of clarifying the counterfactual character of the claims at stake.

11 Meaning, "having been strengthened."

will give you his trove of jades, of turquoises; He will be kind, His heart will be loving. You come from unsophisticated circumstances,[12] you are unfortunate, you go in anguish, you go trembling with cold, shivering, you go about meddling with your word, you go with a dry mouth, and the quality of the eagles, the ocelots swells in vanity.

151. At the thresholds of houses, next to the fences,[13] there you afflict the itty-bitty wood, the pine, the broken chili, the salt grains, there you go with your intestine stuck to you.[14] Then you humbly invoke our Lord. And your mouth waters for a morsel of medicinal herb, a small corn stew thanks to which there is pleasure, there is enjoyment, and your face lights up. Over there is the warmth, the heat of the one who drinks, of the one who eats, who without a face, who without words looks at you; over there you are transformed, you lose heart.

152. With all your effort, your vigor, do it. Go fleeing, running away, sighing; you go about in the ravines, in the hills.[15] Be not upset, grieve not for the sake of our Lord. Only remember His breath, His word over there, because for your sake He came to shine, not only as a flash of precious metal, but as the radiance of turquoise.

For by nothing else will you be enlightened in this way, will you take example. Yet, remember that in this way the Beloved, the beseeched God will make you prosperous here on earth, will make you rejoice. But when He determines, He will send upon you His punishment. You will take refuge, hide, and He will give you, He will show you riches in heaven.

---

12 More literally, the line reads: "You wear *tami* clothing."

13 Meaning, "in the corners."

14 Meaning, "in that case, you go hungry."

15 Meaning, "you live a lost life, that of a savage."

153. And now, my younger brothers, cheer up, rejoice, because the dawn, the daybreak has come upon you; by this be revived, open your eyes with the light, the radiance of the only wonderful God, to whose head and hair no one can reach,[16] because He is the whole principle, the foundation.

And we, whom He has forged, He has shaped us; we are His image, His copies, His human workmanship, we who are captives, we who are scattered in the world, on God's earth.

154. And because of our filth and dust, our stench, our rottenness, we irritated Him, we angered Him, we made Him angry. In that way, no one at His side praised Him, exalted Him, in His house on high, in heaven. Thus, we are only going there, to the place of His embers, to His burning griddle, to His place of stinging nettles, to the devouring land of the owlman, to His oven, to His cavern of fire.

155. And when He looked on us with benevolence, He came to bestow his divinity, the abundance of His turquoise, His breath, His word. That is how He came to polish us, to straighten us, to give us cleanliness. That is how He sent, He commanded, He came to guide those whom He entrusted with the teaching. He made them, the Fathers, say, made them communicate His divine word to those who came to put under His fist.[17] In their bosom, in their throat was placed what they had been guarding, what they had been hiding, namely, the abundance of love, the great goodness of our Lord, so that here they would give protection and shelter, lead and carry people on their shoulders in His land. Yet, for a short time, they will cut us like jewels, they

---

16 Meaning, "whom no one can equal."

17 This phrase is not sinister in Nahuatl but means to be under someone's guard or custodianship.

will polish us like precious stones, by this cleansing, by this straightening of people, by the divine blessing.

156. And receive well, make the divine precepts yours so that I may thus adorn you with jewels, thus put bracelets on your hands, on your feet; so that I may put them on you, bind them within you, place them in your bowels; so that I may give them to you to keep the one who is elevated, the one who is free; so that you may redeem yourself, you who are like a *tami*. When *Dios*, our Lord, sends his stick and stone, his anger, his outrage, his pestilence, then you will protect yourself, you will preserve yourself, you will excel, you will gain in veneration, you will cover yourself with white varnish,[18] you will adorn yourself with feathers; no longer will you come reluctantly to see our Lord; neither will you ignore those whom he entrusted with teaching, those who are mothers, are fathers in divine things, who enlighten us, who explain to us, what they bring near to you.

157. And who are you that you do not take into account their weeping, their tears, that you do not sigh, that you do not moan, that you only shout, that you only yell, that you only go gesticulating, that you only go providing yourself with hallucinating mushrooms, that in this way you disturb, irritate the Fathers, that in this way your foolishness, your inanity scandalizes them?

For *Dios* will dispose you, will bend you down to the edges and corners.[19] He will make you follow the way of the deer and rabbit, will show you the difficult, the heavy. He will make the ravine and precipice your reward, that to which you will be obliged by reason of the very great sin

---

18 Meaning, "you will enjoy the esteem of the ancients."

19 Meaning, "He will make you live in scarcity."

of unbelief. Thus, like dogs, like hens, He will put us under the care of His servants, the Christians,[20] so that we may put our harness, our staff, our metal instrument, our tool to carry to work, since we do not believe in Him, because we are not grateful to those who help us, to those who assist us, who for our sake are tired of talking, who go about twisting their bowels;[21] for our sake they are mortified and suffer.

158. And you will leave those who run about, those who crawl,[22] along with those that begin to bear green ears of corn, those that already bear cornstalk tassels and flowers.[23] On your account will their face and heart, their mount and water be afflicted. Moreover, in the place where the raw materials are, by the walls, the servitude, the tribute work already weighs.

Listen calmly to His breath, to the word of our Lord that, like cold water, like a thin rod is thrown to you so that you can make your own, make your body, follow what is right, the black and red ink,[24] which is the sign of the good children of God.

159. This has been said to you. Not behind you, in back of you, are you to throw it, to kick it, to disdain it. And you should express it, tell it to the people, that you did receive its savor and sweetness from our Lord, that with them you were consoled, that with them your face and heart were bound. Not of happiness, of tranquility were

---

20 An obviously necessary hybridism, which appears as *"Christianome"* in the Nahuatl text.

21 Meaning, "they are suffering hardship."

22 Meaning, "the children."

23 Meaning, "those who are of the age of discretion."

24 The speaker is adapting the native *difrasismo* meaning "what is written," or in an extended sense, reputable knowledge, wisdom.

you deserving. You took advantage of what thus little dripped low to your ear, to your interior, to your moans from the night, to your sighs as a human. In the same way make Him dear to others, make Him heartily desired by others; in the ears of the people, hold them close to Him, by his side, the Lord of heaven, the beloved, the Implored One. Who from across, from the side, has looked at us, blind children. That is all.

Exhortation to those being educated in the church; how they can serve *Dios*, how they will go to confession and how they will prepare themselves for communion

160. Here you are, who receive edification, education; you receive the wing, the tail and wing,[1] to descend and to soar as they do. What do you do? How do you conduct yourself? With what do you occupy yourself? Who perverts the people? Is that the reason you sent your mothers, your fathers to sleep, so that they might be distracted? Because only for that reason have you come, namely, to become worthy, to seek the One by Whom You Live. He placed a word, installed perhaps a lip, perhaps a mouth within you, He, the Lord of the Near and the Nigh; and already that is how you are presumptuous, how you are already proud.

161. What do you do? Does the breath, the word of our Lord make people proud, conceited? Does it not make you weep? Does it not move you that our Lord welcomed you when you went out into the woods, into the overgrowth?[2] Do you not remember it now? What do you do? How do you act? Is that the way of life you lead? Do you already receive warmth and heat? And nowhere do you see the cold, the icy, the misery, that which torments, that which causes distress.

---

1 The line uses the *difrasismo* "*quitlapilli, atlapalli,*" meaning literally "tail, wing," which metaphorically means the "common people" who are guided by the head, the leaders of the people. Yet it is preceded by another synonymous word for "wing" for reasons that are unclear.

2 Meaning, "when you lived like a savage."

Now your mother, your father are no longer. They are no longer there when you call them, when you speak of them.

162. Moreover, perhaps now here it is seen that they take pains for you, they say: "My son went away, he went to do what he should have[3] for me, he went to bring me something to spend the day with." And now, perhaps, will you grant it to your mother, to your father? For you become their torch, their mirror. Do you not remember the one God? Do you direct, lead yourself? Even now bow down, afflict yourself in the house of the Lord of the Near and the Nigh. Where you see Him now, weep, be sad. If you weep, he will show you what you desire, what you seek, because it has been granted to you, because you saw the torch, the mirror, of the One by Whom We Live. Here is He who became mother, who became father. Why don't you respect Him? Why don't you have regard for Him? Are you just how you are? Were you born like that? Did you not come to life? Were you not carried on the backs and backsides of people with their support?

163. And now, sigh, grieve.[4] Perhaps for a short time, perhaps one day, near and nigh to Him you will live; because if you do not give yourself to the house of the Lord of the Near and the Nigh, of the only God, *Dios*, then torment, pain, will appear to you for not dedicating yourself to the home of *Dios*, of the One by Whom We Live; and for not receiving it, for not making it your own, the cold water, the nettle,[5] they are gathered next to you by those who are mothers, fathers,

---

3 The term in Nahuatl, from *macehua*, usually turns on a sense of deserving or meriting.

4 Sighing and weeping was taken to be good behavior, an action to curry the favor of the gods. The present statement looks to be an attempt by Christian clergymen to pull from this metaphorical reservoir.

5 Meaning, "the punishment."

the interpreters of *Dios*. And for this yet weep, grieve, bow down your heads, bow down in humility before the God who is worthy of honor. Perhaps He will show you His warmth and heat, and for a while longer, one more day, you will live in this way.

164. Nevertheless, rejoice in penitence, be happy. And from your breast,[6] here on earth, keep in your heart what you already know, what you already observe. Did you hear it long ago? Did your mothers, your fathers already tell you the word? Why do you not obey your Fathers?[7] Do you dream, do you rise up in haste? Now, let it continue, let the work not finish for he who realizes with intensity, near and nigh to the One by Whom We Live, the one and only God.

165. And now, seek it with affliction, invoke it with tribulation, perhaps what you deserve will amount to something, or perhaps not, for only the word is awaited. And now, distressed in that way, obey the stammerers, the deaf with respect to what we tell you, what we give you. And they give it, they tell it to you—they who are the interpreters of the one God, those who have come to make us grasp the good, the clean, in whose belly, in whose throat the jades, the turquoises have been augmented. He, God, who is everywhere our Lord, *Dios*, truly came to live everywhere on earth. And He comes lavishing, He comes leaving His breath, His glory, His warmth, His softness, His word.

166. And now and sigh, grieve, you are the one who receives edification and education, you go becoming prudent. May you not become proud, haughty, and may you not place it in front of and on top of you[8] for a moment, for one day, when thanks to Him you hear

---

6 Literally, "from your heart," meaning something approximating "voluntarily."

7 In the original Nahuatl, the hybridism *padreme* appears here.

8 Meaning, "I hope you don't underestimate the education you receive."

it, you see it near and nigh to the one who leads, who carries others on his shoulders. May they be thankful for what has happened to you, in that way cry out to our Lord. Now what do you do, how do you act? Have you eaten, drunk so many things,[9] even when you are still a child? Have your eyes, your ears not yet opened? Have you not yet seen? How do you behave, what do you occupy yourself with? Have you thus come to rant, to sleep, to wake up laughing? And since you have come to eat, do you no longer remember where what you eat comes from, who makes it visible, who gives it to you? Is it your mother, your father? No, for it is He, the One by Whom We Live, who is worthy of supplication.

167. And now, be enlivened, observe, for you only blind yourselves, you close your ears. For real, only in your case, what you are taught, what you hear, what you are shown, that by which you truly live for on earth goes right out your ears. And now, may you make yourself worthy. And do penance not only for yourself, but also for him who goes out somewhere, to the forest, to the undergrowth, he who is afflicted with salt and chili,[10] and does not find his sustenance, his livelihood, whose clothing, that which is on his hip, on his neck is scanty. For him you do not weep, you do not grieve. And now, may you not live here before and on top of the people; may you only remember how you will live tomorrow, the day after tomorrow, or one year, two years.

168. What do you do, how do you conduct yourself? May you not be alone like this: in jest, in laughter. May you still speak with affliction to the one, marvelous *Dios*; or else, only devote yourself to what they give you, to what those whom God has taught, the Fathers, tell you, to what they give you, which are like jades, like

---

9 Meaning, "has what is not good, the unwholesome, entered you?"
10 Meaning, "he who finds his food with difficulty."

turquoises. And what do you do? How do you act? Does it not cause you to weep, does it not distress you that you have offended the One God? Do you not understand that we are not righteous? And why is it that you throw, you hurl their admonition there, and only listen but do not do what is good, what is clean? Finally, perhaps you should return there, from where your mothers, your fathers came, perhaps even to that which corrupts, which debases, as it was lived long ago, because here it is known that you have not received His encouragement, His word in the house of our Lord?

169. Moreover, the Fathers, to whom God entrusted the instruction, propose to you, tell you, that there should be concern, dedication to divine things in the house of our Lord, and that you should not be complacent. And therefore our fathers announce to you that our Lord, *Dios*, is already before you, that He loves only the one who is afflicted, who weeps, who is distressed; and He harasses the one who has offended Him in this way, who causes offenses to our Lord before the *padre*;[11] they tell Him everything, they unfold everything before Him, they expose everything that has been done which is not good, not right before Him.

170. And the *padre* said to the people that their beloved friend becomes our Lord, who then becomes their beloved. And you, who on your own abandon Him, you lose him, you do not want to appease our Lord, *Dios*, whoever confesses, whoever uncovers his heart, it is necessary that he hide nothing, that he conceal nothing, that he deny nothing before the One by Whom We Live because, on account of a mortal sin, even if he hides a single word of such a great sin, nothing will disappear of what he did, having committed sins before our Lord, *Dios*.

---

11 The same word, the Spanish *padre*, appears in the original Nahuatl text.

171. Here is another thing that I propose to you, that I say to you, whoever has confessed before *Dios*, whoever has disrobed, whoever before Him, our Lord, has given an account, perhaps he will want to take in, to receive that with which he lives, with which he exists, our Lord Himself, our benefactor, Jesus Christ, who descended upon us and poured out His grace upon us and thus made us His own, rescued us from the hands of our enemies the owlmen. His beloved and marvelous body and his venerated blood, they, together with what is edible, what is drinkable,[12] that is our maintenance, that is what has made his divine nourishment here on earth.

172. Whoever wishes to receive it—even quite early—first, on account of our Lord Jesus Christ, he must attire himself well. And moreover, if he does so not of his own accord, then he will leave his soul, his *anima*, in the hands of his enemy, there, in the Land of the Dead. And now, perhaps a lip, perhaps a mouth, has fallen, has dripped in your ear;[13] with it you will become discerning, thus you observe thanks to the One God, *Dios*. And now make every effort, preserve yourselves thoroughly; do not laugh in that way, do not make jokes, do not mock, not so be scornful of what I have established, of what I have said; be not that way to the stammerer, to the deaf who nowhere do they make the admonition their own. With one lip, two lips, I exhort you, I strengthen you. Now you know; that is all you have heard.

---

12 This can be understood as "our livelihood."

13 Meaning, "you have received and accepted the advice."

Exhortation to those who live in the temple, that they may fully believe in our Lord Jesus Christ, and thus guard his commandments well, as a marvelous thing

173. My beloved children, listen to his encouragement, the word of *Dios*, so that you may become discerning, so that you may observe, so that you may not blindly go to the Land of the Dead. And that this may be shown to you, open your ears, open your hearts, so that the word which I want to set before you may not go out uselessly. Understand the belief in Him, the only One *Dios*, that we live thanks to Him, who created us, made us, and as man redeemed us; only on our behalf did He cause himself to be incarnate, to present Himself as man here on earth. And on our behalf, He suffered, He died on the Cross.[1] That is how He opened the heaven for us that was closed because of our sins.

174. And he who does not believe in the only One *Dios*, our redeemer Jesus Christ, lives only in vain here on earth, for he will only go to the Land of the Dead at the end of his life. So that we may go to heaven and thus enjoy ourselves there forever, He created us, He made us, He feeds us, He gives us life, He takes care of us day by day, always. And whoever does not recognize His redemption of us, the heavenly things that *Dios* wants to give him, when his life ends, he will go to the Land of the Dead, so that there he will burn forever, he will

---

1 This is a hybridism in Nahuatl with *"cruz"* as the root. This is, in Spanish, the term for "cross."

weep, he will hunger, various forms of torment will be rendered upon him. It will be their great misfortune for those who go to the Land of the Dead because there they will forever receive what they deserve, they will suffer in their livelihood, their torment will never end. Therefore, my younger brothers, be discerning, keep the precepts of *Dios*. Love Him with all your heart, with all your strength.

175. And love your neighbors as you love yourselves, for if you do this, you will redeem yourselves, and the owlman, your enemy, will flee before you. Do not strive to follow him. He seeks sins, perhaps by licentiousness, by drunkenness, by theft, perhaps by affliction in order to destroy people's souls,[2] to take them to the Land of the Dead, so that they will not deserve what they have lost on account of their sins. Give your heart to God, that you may rejoice in His house forever, for there He awaits you, for there is your joy.

176. First, my children, I tell you, it is with the word of *Dios* that I wish to tell you, observe in this way so that you may redeem yourselves, so that you may not go to the Land of the Dead where you are always, permanently, afflicted, have regrets, suffer, and are thrown into the fire forever. Open your ears, that not in vain may His breath, the word from the One by Whom We Live, *Dios*, be spoken. And if you hear it well, and keep it well, so will you be redeemed, so will you go to heaven, so will you be there always, permanently pleased, rejoicing, happy, comforted.

177. You see, my children, it is necessary for you to know that only one *Dios* made us, created us, that it is thanks to Him that we live, that He is very much our father, our mother, and that He

---

2 The term used for "soul" here is a form of *yolia*.

is the only one who should be taken as such. Know that there are not two, that there are not three, nor many, as our grandparents used to say a long time ago. That before only one should we bow down with humility, should we kneel, should we take Him as our God. We must consider Him fully as our God because He gives you what is necessary for you, because He always makes our sustenance, our food, our maintenance, with what we live, what we wear, what is necessary for our body. Thus, it is well seen that He is quite worthy of loved, of being sought. Love Him, give Him your heart.

178. Listen, my younger brothers, he who loves *Dios*, does not afflict Him, does not offend Him, lives modestly, does not get drunk, does not commit adultery, does not steal, does not commit murder, does not provoke discord, does not do what is not to be done, what is not good, not right.[3] Instead, he only has a reverential fear of *Dios* and many times acts for, prays to *Dios*, who is everywhere, who lives everywhere, who always watches our hearts, what we are thinking. For this reason, it is always necessary that you separate yourselves with haste from your sins when the *diablo*[4] puts you to the test so that you incur in sins. Do not act so, lest the owlman destroy you, lest he beguile you, lest he take you to the Land of the Dead when you die.

179. Thus, it is necessary that you always seek *Dios* in your reflections. And when you sleep or when you rise you will pray, you will say the *Pater Noster*, *Ave Maria*, *Credo*, *Salva Regina*, in your

---

3 This is an instance of the Christian fathers making use of the *difrasismo* "*in cualli, in yectli.*"

4 The Spanish word *diablo* ("devil") appears in the original text.

language,[5] and you will invoke *Dios* with all your heart, so that He will hear your prayer and give you his *gracia*,[6] you who will be His beloved; so that He will receive you in heaven when you die; so that there, forever, you will rejoice, because He made you so; so that there you will go in glory[7] to His house of rulership. May it be so!

---

5 The names of these prayers appear as such in the original. The friar, however, adds the provision that they may be recited in Nahuatl rather than Spanish or Latin.

6 The term used is *i-gracia-tzin*, a hybridism in Nahuatl and Spanish for, more literally, "revered grace."

7 The original text reads "*in gloria*," which might be a hybrid phrase between Spanish and Nahuatl, but this interpretation would make little sense grammatically. Alternatively, it may also be a phrase entirely in Latin, which is grammatically sensible. This translation reflects the latter option.

Here is what the physician, the one who cures people, is obliged to do, how he should speak to and comfort the sick

180. Physician, healer of people, here is how you should heal and console the sick person who called you to attend him. Your duties are fourfold. The first, which is your greatest duty, is that before you ask him anything, you should say to him, "My son, my dear one, the Lord of the Near and the Nigh has taken you, has seized you, He who is the Owner of the World, the One Whom No One Equals, the One with Whom No One Speaks. He has come to bind you, He has placed you in His cage, in His corner, in the dark. He has placed you at the back of His cage, in His hunting snare.[1] In that way, He has wound you up with His cord, He has put His sickness and pestilence on you. He puts on you the heavy, the harsh, the sickening, His stick and stone, what nothing joins, what nothing conjoins. His nettle and scorpion,[2] He brings them close to you, He puts them in you, thus you become sick."

181. In the second place, my dear friend, I will ask you in this way, and I hope you will answer me well. Now that you are sick, first I tell you that you require it, and it is most necessary that you seek your healer from the people of our Lord God, the confessor, the one who straightens people's hearts, so that you may show Him that which ails you thus, the precious thing which is your *anima*, that which gives you life. Then you will seek to heal your body, if I am able well to heal

---

1 Meaning, "by this illness He is punishing you."
2 A *difrasismo* for punishment.

your heart with Christianity, for you well know that there are two kinds of medicine on earth.

The first, in relation to your body, you will ask God for it with meekness, because you afflicted Him, because you did not reverentially fear Him, if you have committed faults against Him; and you will take into account how much He, our Lord Jesus Christ, will punish the faults of the one who dies with them if he does not confess them on earth. And so, he will weep, so he will be in anguish.

182. The second, if that one does not leave you, that one by which you have thus been attacked, by which you have been bound by the beloved God, the One Worthy of Honor, Jesus Christ, the Peerless One, the One with Whom None Is Equal. All those who are in the world, those who have lived before Him, will be frightened, they will tremble. And you, if you are great, if you know something, perhaps your heart perceives it, dress yourself, act well. Perhaps that is all, perhaps you have caused Him displeasure, perhaps you have caused Him pain, perhaps you have caused affliction to the one who gives protection, to the one who gives help; perhaps He already wants to push you with His foot, He wants to push you away. In the clouds, in the mist, you have already gone about straightening yourself. With your heart make up for it, put in order that by which you thus angered the One by Whom We Live, the One Worthy of Honor, Our Lord Jesus Christ. Gather your sins together, lest His ruin of the people, the owlman come upon you. So, hide some of your sins.

183. And present them to the representative of God, to the padre, so that he may bless you, dispense you from your sins. He will place his hand on you in the name of Dios, so that the offense done to Him, which the owlman drew on you,[3] will disappear. For if you

---

3 Meaning, "that he put in you."

perform well what is here said, then it is said, when you die on earth, you will not die in heaven, though your body dies your soul will not die. In that way will the divine soul, the divine joy live on in the house of God. If here on earth you are prepared, then God will put you in the place of command. And if you go about hiding your faults, you will never be cured; even if your body is cured, your soul will never be cured. Rather, the One by Whom We Live, *Dios*, will punish you there, in the Land of the Dead, forever.

184. The third duty is this. With all your heart hear, know that when we fall sick, we are very much inclined to death because then, together with us, the owlmen come to scatter. Thus, they scatter in expectation of our soul to take it to the Land of the Dead. Therefore, it is quite necessary that with all your heart you kneel down in your intimacy, and join hands with the name of our Lord Jesus Christ. You will invoke Him to redeem you and send His beloved angels[4] to come and wait for your soul as long as it takes to leave, to take it to heaven, to rejoice at the side of *Dios*, our Father.

The fourth is this. Fortunate is he who can redeem himself, if he hears all this that is written here, for he will no longer shrink back in case he dies or is cured; perhaps he will know that he will live. This is how *Dios* admonishes us when we get sick. So may it be on earth!

---

4 In the original text the hybridism *"angelome"* is used.

Exhortation by which people are straightened, telling them how great, how important Christianity and the Christian life are

185. The first thing on which you will speak to your heart[1] is that you are a Christian,[2] therefore, as you are a Christian, so you will reflect with Christian principles; that you are counted among them, all the subjects of *Dios*, who will deserve, will earn the command of heaven so that there, forever, at *Dios*'s side they will reign. And you will also remember, you will speak to your heart on this, that no one, not one of those who are not Christians, will be able to merit the command of heaven.

186. The second thing on which you will speak to your heart, that you will remember is that the name by which you are called, "Christian," is quite wonderful, that it is a quite honorable name because you received it, you took it from the name of Christ, the beloved son of *Dios*, the very true *Dios* and very true man. And thus, you call yourself a Christian, thus you also call yourself a sacred son of *Dios* and you are a younger brother of Jesus Christ. Moreover, your gift is also the

---

1 In this exhortation, the Nahuatl compound phrase for "speak to your heart" is pressed into the service of the Christian understanding of "meditation" and "reflection." A more typical term used among the Nahuas would have been *teomania*, which is not a compound of *yolli* and *notza*, as is found in the present case. The translation retains the awkward neologism.

2 This uses a hybridism, *tiChristiano* in the Nahuatl text. This is generally how the term appears in the text that follows.

command of heaven. This word is written in the Divine Book, St.[3] Paul says it in chapter 8, in the Epistle that he sent to the men of Rome.

187. My younger brothers, men of Rome, you are already Christians. Know that you are already children of *Dios*, who has already made you his sacred children. This word is strengthened and verified by the Holy Spirit, who thus tells us the straight truth in our inner being; and He never lies, He can never lie. And it is so already, it is certain already that we are the sacred children of *Dios*, and only thus is it also ours, is the lordship of *Dios* our gift; and His present is for us, for all, namely the mercy from Jesus Christ, as His gift, which belongs to Him. And in this He is the first, He leads the command of heaven. So too will all good Christians be in heaven.

188. This divine word is well seen, well recognized as a very great gift, as a great act of mercy, which all the Christians obtained, received by reason of the sacred wetting of the head, baptism,[4] because they took the name by which they call themselves Christians from Him, they took the name of Christ; and their father is Christ Himself, and His command of them is the same command of Christ which will always be, will never finish, will never end.

---

3 Abbreviated in the original Nahuatl.
4 This is the Nahuatl neologism *"Paptismo."*

Talk explaining that it is a great distinction, a great honor, to receive the Holy Baptism, the wetting of the head

189. My younger brother, Christian, it is necessary that you often speak to your heart on what is quite great, on the quite remarkable distinction, on the renown that was produced for you when you were exalted with the wetting of the head, the baptism,[1] because that, as when you had not yet received it, when in you the wetting of the head was not yet done, you were damaged, harmed, you were *tzitzimimitl*,[2] *Satanas*;[3] and within you the *tzitzimimitl* was in your *anima*; and moreover, your *anima* was in darkness, in shadows, and with suffering you consoled yourselves, you endured sickness.

190. And when you had your wetting of the head, then He who redeems us, Jesus Christ, dwelt within you, in your *anima*; and also, then, He illumined it with His divine light and soothed it with His grace[4] and made it His child; and, moreover, it became His accompanying gift. So, much is required of you that you make all your effort, that is how you will take care of it. You should not take it out, so that you do not harass Him, the Lord who is superior in everything, within your soul. Also, you should take much care not to lose it, lest you waste the very great wealth which is His grace. And so that you

---

1 This uses the unaltered Spanish term *Baptimo* in the Nahuatl text.

2 A mythical and maleficent being.

3 In the original Nahuatl the term appears in Spanish, meaning "Satan."

4 A hybridism in the original, using *gracia*. So, it is with all later instances of "grace" in this discourse.

may act, so that you may work in the many things required of you; you shall go behind Him, you shall follow His path, I mean to say, how He lived on earth, that He never incurred sins, that He paid His tribute. It is also required of you that as long as you live on earth you will not spend your time in dissipations, you will not engage in committing sins. All that has been mentioned, everything, is written in the Divine Book, thus St. Paul expressed it in chapter 3;[5] it was his letter which he sent to the men of Galatia.

191. All of you who have wet your heads, there, in the divine house of the one who redeemed us, Christ. You have wrapped yourselves, you have tied on his garment, the garment of our protector, Jesus Christ. This is to say that you have promised that all the time you live on earth, you will never sin, you will never act sinfully; and your promise was made and so you should keep it. In that way, you will take care of His grace, the one He gave you, the one He offered you as a gift in the divine wetting of the head, the baptism.

192. And this, the grace of *Dios*, cannot be kept, cannot be cared for, unless it is well guarded, unless effort is made, unless there is attachment to the commandments of *Dios*, and unless he who does not obey them is shunned, abandoned, and alluded to with fear for all his mortal sins. About this also thus says David in Psalm 29: "Our Lord, my affliction, my sorrow, thou hast changed them into my joy, into my consolation; and thou hast split my burden in half, and hast induced me to joy, to cheerfulness, and so hast led me on every side, with joy, with contentment."[6]

---

5 Abbreviated in the original.

6 Notably, this does not match the contents of Psalm 29. They match verses 11–12 of Psalm 30 more closely. Those read: "(11) You turned my wailing into dancing; you

193.

These words—it is necessary for the Christian to say every day, and thus to show gratitude, to acknowledge the favor, the mercy with which he was helped by the wetting of his head, because before he was burdened with sorrow, weeping, and tears because of his sins. And so, *Dios* filled him with his grace, and with joy and contentment. And before thus he was wrapped up in sins as if they were his garment—as a very hard bundle, which hurts much, so he had it on—and the garment of Him who redeemed us, Jesus Christ, was given to him, was bound to him. Because of that, the belief, it is quite necessary that he should cherish whoever has wetted his head and firmly believes in it. And it is still quite necessary that he should die believing in it and not abandon it. Thus, much is required that he should believe freely, that is,[7] that he should believe in it for himself.

194.

It is not only necessary that you believe in all that our mother, the Holy Church[8] believes, you should also believe in all that is referred to, that which is articulated, that which is worthy of belief, that which is explained by the wise men in the divine word, and in as many things as it is necessary to believe. Then your heart will be satisfied, then you will see.

---

removed my sackcloth and clothed me with joy, (12) that my heart may sing your praises and not be silent. Lord my God, I will praise you forever."

7 Abbreviated in the original.

8 In Spanish in the original.

Talk in which it is explained how it is very great, very honorable that we have been helped by the loving suffering and the loving death of our God, our Lord Jesus Christ

195. You should take great care to remember and speak to your heart about your own risk, about the danger you were in when you had not yet wet your head. You must know that you were in the hands of the owlman, of the *tzitzimimitl*, and that if you had died when you had not yet wet your head, the *diablo* would have taken you there, to the Land of the Dead, there where you would have always, permanently, perpetually suffered. You would have paid the penalty with diverse and hard sufferings, torments, pains. And because of the quite great, quite dreadful character of your perishing, of your risk, the Lord Jesus Christ redeemed you, protected you. And with this, because of His beloved blood, His glory, His death, and His suffering, this is a fruit that you have received, from which you have profited, by the wetting of your head.

196. This which has been said is written in the divine book. This is how St. Paul articulated it in the letter he wrote to the men of Rome, in chapter 6: "You Romans, my brethren, who have wet your heads, you know well, you recognize with certainty that by this wetting we were separated, marked, and all our sins were erased; and because the grace of *Dios* was given to us and with forgiveness we became his children with his protection." This is a very great, a very honorable gift that came from Him, for which we should be grateful—for the death and suffering of our Lord Jesus Christ.

197. For this reason, and the many favors he did us, it is necessary that we love Him, that we honor Him and cherish

Him. And it is also necessary that we, daily, remember this fully good death from which came the very great favor and act of compassion. And in that way our heart can always be at his side so that we may always remember well our mother Holy Church,[1] the one who guides, the one who leads us to Our Lord, the Holy Spirit, the one who arranged that day by day, Mass or Masses be said everywhere in the churches, because the Mass is His remembrance, because in it we remember his death and the sufferings of the one who redeemed us; because He Himself—the true *Dios*, the true man who is always there, the one who always makes and gives the people joy—is there, in the Blessed Sacrament.

198. But moreover, not only by all that was this death and suffering beneficial, but also by His mercy and compassion for our *animae*,[2] for our souls. For by that we are also indebted, we received the gift of our body. Because our body, with the beloved fruit, with its honor, will grow and it will be remade, begotten, born again so that forever, permanently, over there, living in heaven. With heavenly joy we will go about desiring that, we will go about waiting for it.

199. But we shall put it[3] well in our hearts and remember it for that is how we may well merit this very great and wonderful heavenly joy and prosperity. Much is required of us that we take care of it so that we may know Dios well, with firm faith, and in that way be able to love Him with right, divine love. In that way, we will keep His divine command and thus obey our mother Holy Church. And that is

---

1 The "Holy Church" portion of this phrase is in Spanish in the original. The same holds for the following phrases in this passage: "Mass / *missa*," "Holy Spirit / *Spiritu Sancto*," and "Most Sacred Sacrament / *Sanctissimo Sacramento*."

2 The original contains a trilingual hybridism among Nahuatl, Spanish, and Latin, "*tanimas*."

3 The pronoun refers to the message from Paul's Epistle to the Romans, chapter 6.

how we will be prudent, guard ourselves from all mortal sins, and abhor, confront our enemies in the world and the owlman—later, in addition to that, our flesh. About this St. Paul, who wrote a letter to the men of Rome, speaks. In chapter 6 he says to them: "My younger brothers, men of Rome,[4] know that by the wetting of the head we died and were buried with him who redeemed us, Christ; for also by the wetting of the head alone we committed ourselves to abhor the world, and all its fame, its wonders, its vanity."

200. And we also have committed to reject the owlman's slander, his mockery, his fun at the expense of the people. And so, with all the sins, in that way to cast out, to tear away his greed, his ambition from our flesh. For this, on account of sins, we thus die, and on account of Christ's sake, we live. If we do this of our own hearts[5] for all the time we are here on earth, we will live at His side, together with our Lord Jesus Christ. There, in our father, *Dios's* house of command, we will merit, we will attain His joy, His jubilation for our body and *anima*.

201. For this reason St. Paul too, in the same chapter says to the men of Rome: "If we imitate Him, if we fulfill our obligations to our Lord Jesus Christ, we shall die as He did, and so shall we be buried with Him, for we shall also appear in the resurrection." This, which is still its primary meaning, means to say that by the wetting of one's head we die with Christ and are buried with Him. In this way, our works, and our thoughts, and our words are all made quite visible.

---

4 Although a similar greeting to the one above in paragraph 196, the Nahuatl is different.

5 This the typical Nahuatl phrase used by the Church fathers to express "our free will," namely "*toyollocopa*."

Only by reason of all this will the service and obedience to Jesus Christ be made visible.

202. And we shall be of no service to the world, nor to the owlman, nor to our flesh. Quite well, in that way, shall we know that we shall die and be buried. Those who wish to scorn everything from the world, the *diablo*, and the flesh, will pay their tribute well if they make the divine commandments a part of their lives.

This is all there is to hear. Believe in it well, you who are a Christian. Take it well, firmly; keep it well and make it part of your life; commit your heart and put your efforts into it because it is what gives life, vivifies. And if you guard it, if you make it part of your way of life, it will be what you deserve, your gift, a permanent joy. May it be done!

In some other time, the name of the Lord was praised, our Lord Jesus Christ, the true *Dios* and true man.

Part II

SOCIAL ROLE
DESCRIPTIONS

Priests, Astronomers, and Philosophers

(Coloquios y Doctrina Cristiana, *fol. 3r–v, 96–97*)

Introduction[1]   Also, our lords,
there are also those who guide us,
who carry us, who support us,
who show how to serve our gods,
whose servants, whose tail and wing,[2] we are.

Priest   There are those priests who make the offerings, who
burn incense,
and those priests called Quequetzalcoa.[3]
There are those who know of discourses,[4]
and their office is to be concerned,
all night and all day,
with putting on copal,
with their burnt offerings,
with the thorns to draw blood.

---

1 All the terms in this left-hand column are introduced for the purposes of clarification and are not present in the Nahuatl text.

2 The phrase "tail and wing" is a *difrasismo* often used to distinguish the common class of people from nobility. In this context, it is used to distinguish humans from divine nature.

3 *Quetzalcoatl* is the title of the highest-ranking priests or pontiffs among the Nahuas. The *Códice Matritense de la Academia*, fol. 119r ff., indicates more than thirty distinct classes of priests.

4 *Tlatol-mati-ni-me*, the term here in the original, means literally the plural (*me*) of one who (*ni*) knows (*mati*) discourses (*tlatolli*). It is thus etymologically related to

Astronomers	There are those who see, who are concerned with the course and ordered process of the sky, how the night is divided.
Philosophers	And there are those who read, those who count, those who loudly turn the pages of the codices, Those who have in their power the black and red ink and what is painted. They accompany us, guide us, make us speak upon the path.[5]
Day-Sign Readers	There are those who order how a year goes, how the count of day-signs[6] and each of the months follow their path. They are concerned with these matters, to them is entrusted the task of speaking about the divine.

---

the term for the philosopher, the *tla-mati-ni*, but is restricted to knowledge of what is in discourses, *tlatol(li)*.

5 The term used here, *tech-oh-tlatol-tia*, means literally they cause (*tia*) us (*tech*) to be told about matters (*tlatol*) of the path (*oh*). Recall, from the Introduction that the Nahua path is a conception of justice in general.

6 The term used here, *tonal-pohual-li*, is the count (*pohua*) for a day's date (*tonal*), like Wednesday the 14th, the sort of energy thought to be distributed by the sun, and one's destiny, if born on that day. The calendar under discussion, however, is the 260-day "ritual" calendar. It was composed by cycling through the full combination of 13-day sequences and 20-day sequences. The Nahuas also had a 365-day solar calendar, which would not be the source of discussion in this passage.

The Philosopher: *Tlamatini*

(Florentine Codex, *vol. 10, ch. 8, pp. 29–30*)

The philosopher is a torch, a stout lit torch.

He[7] is a mirror, a wide mirror pierced on both sides.

He is forged by the tradition stored in books of black and red ink.

He *is* the ink of black and red;[8] is a path,

a leader of people,[9]

a rower, a guide, a companion, an achiever.

Like a watchful physician, the good philosopher is a reputable person
of trust, and a credible teacher worthy of confidence.

He is a counselor and a coach,

fostering sound judgment in others.

---

7 Most philosophers were certainly male, but women could be philosophers too.
The Lady of Tula, for example, was of common birth but made her way to the royal
court of Tetzcoco as a *tlamatini*. For a description of her wisdom, see the colonial
historian Ixtlilxochitl's account in vol. 2 of his *Obras históricas*, 268.

8 What is written in red and black ink, in *amoxtli* (the screen-folded, pre-
Columbian logographic books), is what is recorded as history and tradition. The
grammar of the sentence means that the philosopher is the living embodiment of
traditional knowledge and what is right.

9 The relationship between philosophers and their ability to lead people, then, was
close. Passages describing the role of the king—for example, the passage in *Florentine Codex*, vol. 6, ch. 4, p. 17—suggest that an ideal king needed many of the same
qualities of character, especially the ability to know one's self. Plato's suggestion,
in *Republic* IV, 484a–502c would not have been preposterous, but common sense
among the Nahuas.

He informs one's mind and clarifies, acting as a guide, preparing
    one's path.
And he goes accompanying one, teaching one to know oneself.

Like a physician, he is worthy of being taken as an example,
effectively arranging affairs and establishing order.
He illuminates the world and knows what is above and below
    the earth.[10]
He is serious and dignified, revered by his descendants,
and a person with whom one is strengthened.
He is confided in, trusted, quite affable,
satisfying one's heart, making one content,
and like a helpful physician, empathizes with one.

Like a stupid physician, the bad philosopher is imprudent.
He claims to know divine matters and boasts falsely and vaingloriously.
He pretends to be wise, boasts vainly, and is disgraced.[11]
He is a lover of the obscure and the edge.
Like a [bad][12] mystery worker, soothsayer, or physician, he steals from
    the public.

---

10 *Tepan mictlan onmati*, the phrase in the original, literally reads: "She knows what
is above and below [the realm where we live, i.e. the earth]." This is philosophically
interesting, since one charge against Socrates, and for which he was put to death,
was that he claimed to know what was above and below the earth (*Apology* 19b).

11 "*Atoiatl, tepexitl*" literally means a river, a rocky place, but functions here as a
difrasismo for disgrace. Compare Miguel León-Portilla's explanation in *La filosofía
náhuatl*, ch. 1, fn27.

12 The brackets (here and throughout part II) indicate that this is an addition of
the translation, suggested by context. Scholars divide sharply on this point.

Like a [bad] soothsayer, he is one who disorients others, misleads them,
  destroys their judgment.
He makes difficulties for them and leads them into dangerous
  situations.
He causes others to die, destroys people, devastates land, and mysteriously ends up better off.[13]

The Craftsman: *Toltecatl*[14]
(*Florentine Codex, vol. 10, ch. 7, p. 25*)

The craftsman is learned;[15] is an artisan. There were many of them.

The good craftsman is one who is useful and able, adroit,[16]
  diligent, reflective.

---

13 These last lines are difficult to translate without an holistic interpretation. Dibble and Anderson, in their translation of vol. 10 of the *Florentine Codex*, take the
description to suffer Christian interpolations, so that *nahualli, tlapouhqui* and the
like are taken as paradigm examples of bad people. On this line of reasoning, the bad
philosopher is likened to them because of an association with powers that Sahagún
and his informants thought to be from the Devil (Sahagún was the Spanish clergy-
man and principal compiler of the *Florentine Codex*). The approach represented in
this translation does not take this view, but rather, following León-Portilla, seeks to
make sense of the terms in a way that is consistent with the view that what is present in these lines is a coherent philosophical statement.

14 The translation retains the masculine gender because the persons in this role
would have been men exclusively.

15 The term used in the original is *tlamachtilli,* which is related to *mati,* "to know."
The craftsman, then, is a kind of knower, but the passage will indicate that his form
of knowledge is primarily that of skilled experience, *imati.*

16 The term used here is *mimati,* a form of *imati.*

The good craftsman is one who is eager, who is patient, who is calm
in work.

He works from care, [and] makes items of skill.

He crafts, prepares, makes, orders, joins, arranges materials.

The foolish[17] craftsman is one who works carelessly.

He is one who deceives, who steals, who defrauds.

He acts carelessly, deceives others. He is a thief.

The Mystery Worker: *Nahualli*

(Florentine Codex, *vol. 10, ch. 9, p. 31*)

The mystery worker[18] is one who is wise,[19] who is a confidant and
is trusted.

He is serious, a person of authority, worthy of being feared, unflappable,
unreviled, beyond reproach.

The good mystery worker is one who is a lookout, who is calm, and
a guardian.

---

17 The passage is unusual since it breaks the structure of comparing a good x and a
bad x. In this case, one has *xolopitli*, someone with poor judgment.

18 Dibble and Anderson give this person the title "sorcerer" and Shagagún labels
them "*brujos y hechicros*," i.e., "witches and magicians." Yet, these terms leave no
room for any positive dimension to this character's activity. To leave that dimension open, I have instead settled on the more neutral "mystery worker."

19 Importantly, the mystery worker is described as a *tlamatini*, the same term used
for a philosopher. The context of the passage, however, shows that the matters (*tla*)
about which he knows (*mati*) are comparably restricted in content and focus.

He is one who is aware and alert, caring for and helping out with matters.
Never does he harm anyone.

The bad mystery worker is one who does [bad] things.
He is an enchanter, one who casts spells on others to fall in love.
He corrupts their character.[20]
He casts spells over people, curses them, makes them
become possessed.[21]
He deceives and confuses people.

The Soothsayer, Reader of Days:
Tlapouhqui, Tonalpouhqui[22]
(Florentine Codex, vol. 10, ch. 9, p. 31)

The soothsayer is a wise person,[23] one who has books and writings.

The good soothsayer is one who reads the days for another.

---

20 Literally, he turns their hearts, he turns their faces. The *difrasismo* at work here
is *yollotl, ixtli.*

21 Literally, he makes them into *tlacatecolotl*, owlmen. Since these are people who
were thought to change form into animals, this translation follows Dibble and
Anderson in glossing it as a form of possession.

22 Literally, only *tonalpouhqui* means one who (*qui*) reads (*pouh*) days (*tonal*). The
other term, *tlapouhqui*, means only one who (*qui*) counts or reads (*pouh*) things
(*tla*). The juxtaposition in the title is meant to indicate that they are, for the present
context, equivalent terms.

23 The term used here is again *tlamatini*, literally one who knows things. The context of the passage makes clear, however, that the generality at stake is not that of
the philosopher.

He reviews and recalls their meaning.

He reads the days and brings their meaning to one's attention.

The bad soothsayer[24] is one who lies to people, who deceives them.

He is one who speaks falsely, in the way of a [bad] mystery worker, in the way that an owlman speaks, in the way that causes harm to people.

He confuses, distracts, lies, deceives.

---

24 The text looks to be mistranscribed. It reads, literally, *tlacateculotl*, but the likely intention is *tlapouhqui*. Otherwise, a description of the *tlapouhqui* would be incomplete, and the *tlacatecolotl* of the next section would be preceded by a description of the bad version before even the general description was given.

The Owlman: *Tlacatecolotl*[25]

(Florentine Codex, vol. 10, ch. 9, pp. 31–32)

The owlman[26] is one who transforms himself, who is a mystery worker.[27]

He causes harm to people, destroys them, he implants them with illness.

He is one who bleeds himself over people, makes people drink potions

    kills them that way.

He burns representative figurines of others.[28]

There is want and hunger in his home. [29]

Severe affliction is what he deserves, is his reward.

He is poor, wretched, useless, without resources.

---

25 Technically, *tecolotl* is a horned owl. There is much in this passage that is still puzzling for Nahua scholars.

26 Sahagún departs quite widely from the Nahuatl text, writing: *"El hombre que tiene pacto con el demonio se transfigura en diversos animales* / The man who made a pact with the devil and transforms himself into various animals" (*Historia de las cosas de Nueva España*, 538). There is no mention of a pact with the devil in the Nahuatl text. The passage also breaks with the standard approach: general description of *x*, the good *x*, the bad *x*. The scholarly question, then, is whether these owlmen were strictly mystery workers for evil, or whether it was Sahagún's hand that portrays them so. The owl (*tecolotl*) was generally associated with the underworld, *Mictlan*, the Land of the Dead, but this was not an inherently bad place; it was not the Christian Hell. For further development of the figure, see López Austin (1967).

27 The description, then, depicts the owlman as a special kind of mystery worker, and so one class of *tlamatini*. This is why I have included it in this section on knowledge workers.

28 Accepting, clearly, Dibble and Anderson's interpretation, which follows Eduard Seler's (1963) and Sahagún's observations.

29 Sahagún inserts a causal relationship into his translation, so that it reads "because of this. . . . " That is not present in the Nahuatl. It is not clear, then, if his poverty is thought to be a punishment for his bad actions. A Christian view tends to see bad actions as recompensed in this way, but it is not clear if the Nahuas did.

He lives with rags on his neck and hips.

He is fatigued and lives with great need on the slippery earth.

He makes one possessed, he destroys people, he burns representative
figurines of them.

He bleeds himself over people, destroys them mysteriously, steps on
their hearts.

He transforms himself into a dog, bird, a screech owl, an owl, a horned owl.

The Brave Man: *Oquichtli*[30]

(Florentine Codex, *vol. 6, ch. 6, p. 23*)

The brave man is tall, quite tall, small, fat, thin, quite fat, quite thin, a
little like a stone pillar, capable, handsome.

The man of eagles and jaguars[31] is scarred, painted.

He is strong hearted, firm hearted, rock hearted.

The good, the true, brave man is one who stands as a man, resolute,
who charges and who strikes the enemy.

He stands as a man, making his heart resolute and firm, he charges, he
strikes at the enemy.

None does he fear. None meet his gaze.

---

30 Literally, "man." Yet, in this case, the term functions by synecdoche to stand
in for bravery, just as *virtus* in Latin derives from *vir* and *andreia* in Greek derives
from *anēr*.

31 This line compounds the *difrasismo* used to indicate both bravery and the station of warriors, *in quauhtli, in ocelotl* with the term for "man / husband," *oquichtli*,
to give one *in oquichquauhtli ocelutl*. It makes clear, then, that the sort of man under
discussion is the brave man. The term *oquichtli* thus functions in Nahuatl in some
cases as a metonym for bravery, as *andreia* did for the Greeks.

The bad brave man is one who leads others to destruction by deception,
who by deception puts one into difficulty.

He is one who concerns himself with other houses.

He is one who shouts, who petulantly kills others, who forsakes one.

He is one who pisses himself with fear, becomes a coward, and urinates
from fear.

He puts one in difficulty by deception.

The Ruler: *Tlahtoani*[32]

(Florentine Codex, *vol. 10, ch. 4, p. 15*)

The ruler provides shelter, is a great, full cypress tree.

He is fierce, worthy of being obeyed, honored, esteemed, of good
   repute, renowned.

The good ruler is a protector, one who embraces[33] [his subjects] with
   his arms, who unites, gathers, and collects them.

He rules, bears the load for the property.

He embraces his subjects with his cape.

He governs and is obeyed.

The people have recourse to him as a place of shade and shelter.

He serves as a proxy as a representative.

The bad ruler is a savage beast, an air demon, a demon, a jaguar, a wolf.

He is one who is infamous, who is to be left alone, avoided. He
   respects nothing.

---

32 The Nahuatl terms for principal male and female nobles do not precisely line up,
in part because the Nahuas employed a wide range of terms that have no equivalent in English, and in part because women could not hold the positions of highest
political rank.

33 These terms used to describe the good ruler are identical to those used in
describing the father. The relationship between a father and a great ruler, then, is
conceived to be quite close.

He has a damaged character.[34]
He instills and spreads fear.
He is wished dead.

A Lady: *Cihuatecuhtli*

(Florentine Codex, *vol. 10, ch. 13, p. 46*)

The lady is a careful administrator, sympathetic, a provider.
She is worthy of being obeyed, serious, worthy of service.
She is one who manages an estate, who bears the burden.
[She is] famous, illustrious, renowned.

The good lady is one who is patient, who is calm, who is empathetic
She is humane, one who supports another.
She is one who is rock hearted, who is resolute, who endures bravely,[35]
    who abhors turpitude.
She guides her estate, governs people, leads them.
She provides livelihood for people, arranges matters well, tranquilly
    administers for peace.

---

34 More literally, "wild hearted and damage-faced."

35 The terms used here, beyond bravely enduring (*tla-oquich-huia-ni*), include *iollo-tetl*, rock hearted, and *iollo-chichic*, more literally, bitter hearted. They appear in the description of the brave person (see above) and ruler's speech to the inhabitants of his city, where the magnanimous person is depicted as the cypress tree (*Florentine Codex*, vol. 6, ch. 14, p. 73). This point supports the view that the central qualities of bravery find a wider range of application beyond their core meaning on the battlefield.

The bad lady is one who is rash, who is fitful.

She incites riots, causes, instills, and spreads fear. She terrorizes as if she ate people.

She makes people flee, inflicting great harm on people.

She is wasteful.

The Bad Youth: *Telpochtlahueliloc*[36]
(Florentine Codex, *vol. 10, ch. 8, p. 37*)

The bad youth has a bad heart.

He goes about drinking crude wine. He is one who sets a bad example,[37] is foolish, is greatly afflicted, a drunk, a sot.

He goes about eating mushrooms. He goes about deranged.

He is one who is anxious, shameless, obscene, dressed inappropriately, talking about what he should not.

He is impertinently hearted, twist hearted, bitter hearted.

He is without what is precious; consumes his inner substance.

He is vain, full of himself.

He is one who seeks pleasure, a libertine, one who leads a life of, goes out for pleasure.

---

36 Sahagún translates this term as *alcahuete*, meaning "pimp," though nothing resembling the managing of prostitutes appears in the passage. Dibble and Anderson thus prefer "lewd youth," but again, nothing in the passage suggests this either. The passage, moreover, covers more than sexual matters, so this translation chooses a neutral title.

37 The term used, *miuintiani*, is also another term for a drunk. The broader meaning is presented in this translation, but both could be intended.

[His life] is dirtied, filled with excrement, filled with dust and filth.
He is one with a consort, a talker. He takes a concubine, lives
   for pleasure.

The Bad Married Woman: *Tetzauhcihuatl*

(Florentine Codex, *vol. 10, ch. 15, p. 56*)

The bad[38] married woman is one who destroys [relationships], one who
   dissimulates [in her relationships].[39]
She is frivolous, [deserving of] ridicule, laughter, mockery.
She is without name or father, as if she were dead, deceased.
She bears bastards.
She one who aborts.[40]
No one deals with her.

---

38 Note that the term used for "bad" in the present case is not "-*tlahueliloc*," but
"*tetzauh-*," which Dibble and Anderson choose to render "scandalous" on account
of the contents of the following passage. A feature of the grammar that cannot be
rendered well in English is that in this case "badness" or "scandal-riddenness" is the
class into which the woman is said to fall, while in the other cases, the general class
is that of the "youth" or "old man," which is then differentiated by the bad quality
that is their characteristic.

39 Effectively, she is the one who "cheats" or commits "adultery," but it is worth
noting that the Nahua concepts do not evoke breaking the rules of a game, "cheat-
ing," or polluting a relationship, "adultery." They turn rather on breaking up what is
together, to shaving them apart.

40 It is not clear from this passage whether she aborts children or her relationships.
Later, a form of *tlaxilia* is used in the context of aborting relationships, and so serves
a synonym for adultery.

She commits adultery, practices adultery.[41]

She casts off, deceives, and blinds [her husband].

The Bad Old Man: Huehuetlahueliloc[42]

(Florentine Codex, vol. 10, ch. 8, p. 37)

The bad old man has no reputation, no family name.

He goes out for pleasure, is an old pleasure seeker.

He is a decrepit old man, feeble, quite decrepit.

He goes out for pleasure, becomes an old pleasure seeker.[43]

He is a decrepit and feeble old man who is a pervert.

---

41 Again, the Nahuatl concept, *tetlaxima*, has nothing to do with pollution, instead being a matter of scraping or shaving. The idea, like *"tepania,"* appears to turn on literally superficial activities, i.e., deceptive ones.

42 Sahagún chooses *embaucadores* or "tricksters," while Dibble and Anderson choose "the old whoremonger." The latter is at least closer to the description of the passage. One almost wonders whether the more colloquial "creepy old guy" might prove most apt.

43 The causative interpretation of Sahagún's quite loose translation is an interesting one. On that rendering, which Dibble and Anderson do not follow, this is the sort of person who bewitches others to act for their own ends.

The Pleasure Woman: *Ahuiani*[44]

(Primeros Memoriales, *fol. 59r, col. A, 216–17*)

The twelfth paragraph, in which the names of the bad women, the pleasure women, are stated.

You are a pleasure woman.
Pleasure woman.

You scorn others.
You are a loner.
You are shameless.[45]
You have a big itching bum.

You go about[46] summoning people by nodding.
You go about smiling at people.
You go about sticking your tongue out at people.
You go about whistling at people using your mouth.

---

44 This term identifies a social role, while the prostitute is more literally one who sells her flesh, *monamacac*. One finds a description of this person among the cholate and tobacco sellers in the *Florentine Codex* (vol. 10, ch. 26, p. 94), since she is one who sells her own "meat."

45 The translation accepts the correction of *ticuecuetzoc* for *tzicuecuetztoc*.

46 In this passage the term *nemi* is often compounded with others. It means, most often, "to live." But it has that meaning because it meant originally "to move about." The translations that follow, then, sometimes use "go about" and sometimes "live" or "lead your life," but in both cases it is the same term in Nahuatl.

You go about whistling at people using your hand.
You go about summoning people using your hand.

You go about feeling people's genitals.
You go about permitting sodomy.[47]
You are a shameless woman.

You are a shameless girl.
You are a bad woman.
You live in excess.

You go about painted with cochineal.
You go about kicking things.
You go about dragging things.
You go about chewing gum.

You lead your life on the [wrong] path.
You are proud.[48]
You live haughtily.

---

47 This looks to be a new term in Nahuatl formed in what James Lockhart has called stage two texts. The term for "sodomite," *cuiloni*, is related to the term for a scribe, *tlacuilo* (adding the "*ni*" to form an agent noun). The metaphor, then, is to dip one's "pen" into another. Of course, the Christian notion of sodomy was quite variable in its time also, as Mark Jordan (1997) ably shows. It is difficult, then, to know for sure whether a specific sexual act was intended, or whether only illicit sexual activity, in a general sense, is intended. Moreover, one wonders how much Christian influence is at work in these passages.

48 Literally, in this line, "you hold your head high," and in the next, you live "your life with your head held high." This is the opposite of the virtue of humility, *tololiztli*, which is to bow one's head.

You are without tranquility.
You are of no one's house.[49]

You are a seducer of people.
You turn people's hearts.
You summon people in secrecy.

You go about laughing at people.
You go about joking with people.
You wander about the market.

---

49 Literally, you do not (a) see (ita) your (mo) home (chan). Parallel passages about life on the wrong path, for example in the present book's *Discourses of the Elders*, suggest that the person lives not as part of someone's house (see par. 34–36). This means not that they are homeless in a contemporary sense, but without the guard or protection of a family and *calpolli* structure.

Acknowledgments

I express my gratitude to David Bowles, who graciously offered to read the present translation and tell me where and why he thought I was wrong; to the work's editors at W. W. Norton, Alane Mason, Mo Christ, Bob Byrne, who ensured that this work achieved what it could; to my agent Esmond Harmsworth, who pushed to get this idea into print; to Sally Davies for believing that a philosophical discussion about the Aztecs in public venues was needed at all; to the many, many philosophers who directly encouraged the completion of this work, including Andrew Fitz-Gibbon, Mecke Nagel, Nikolay Karkov, Walter Mignolo, Lewis Gordon, and Bryan van Norden; to James Maffie and Alexus McLeod for their early support and honest assessments of my philosophical ideas; and above all to Elyse, my wife and fellow philosopher who not only tells me when I'm wrong, but who also supports me in pursuing what is both beautiful and difficult.

Philosophical Glossary

This glossary is not intended as a replacement for a dictionary. It presents, first, the typical translation, then how the term is often rendered in the text for philosophical purposes. Finally, if necessary, some explanation for the philosophical context is provided.

ahuiya "To be happy or contented." The translation renders this term "contented," to distinguish it from *paqui*, which also means "to become happy" but in the sense of experiencing pleasure or enjoyment. "Ahuiya" is also to be distinguished from *huellamati*, which has been rendered as "joyful."

atl, tepetl "Water" and "hill, mountain, or precipice." Taken together they may form a *difrasismo* for a city, its surrounding land, and its political organization. The term "altepetl" is a contraction of the *difrasismo* and its own word meaning the same thing as the longer phrase. The translation renders the *difrasismo* it "mount and water" for aesthetic reasons.

atoyatl, tepexitl   "A river, current, torrent, stream." "A precipice, large rock, precipice, ravine." Taken as a locative *difrasismo* the pair of terms are used in contexts metaphorically to denote a place of moral danger and difficulty—one of moral straits.

cententli, cencamatl   "One lip." "One mouth." The metaphorical suggestion appears to be what passes between one's lips, through the breach in one's mouth. Together, these terms form a *difrasismo* for a word, or in an extended sense, a thought or doctrine.

cozcatl, quetzalli   "Necklace, jewel, ornament." "A quetzal feather," which would be from the long green tail of a trogon bird. Taken together, the terms form a *difrasismo* for sons and daughters.

cua   Also spelled *qua*. It means "to eat, to bite." When made an object noun, it becomes *cualli*, which means "respectful, a polite person, or a good thing" in an ethical sense. The metaphorical connection appears to be that something *cualli* is what can be absorbed which makes one well. Some passages that discuss eating, then, may also be discussing goodness in a metaphorical way. It is sometimes translated in this work as "wholesome."

cualli, yectli   Also spelled *qualli, yectli*; see individual explanations of these terms. Taken together, they form a *difrasismo* meaning excellence or virtue.

cueitl, huipilli   "A skirt." "A blouse." Because these were the typical clothes of women, they function as a *difrasismo* to mean a woman or wife.

cuitlapilli, atlapalli
"A tail." "A bird wing." Taken together they form a *difrasismo* for the common people as opposed to the nobles, who, presumably, form the head of the bird. The metaphorical suggestion for the body politic is thus conceived as a bird that flies only with the presence and cooperation of all parts.

huehuetque, ilamatque
"An old man." "An old woman." When addressed reverentially, these terms often form a *difrasismo* for one's ancestors.

icac
"To be standing." In an ethical context of this work, it is one of the metaphorical terms used to discuss the good life. It is the way by which one stands on the (slippery) earth. See *tlalticpac* for more context.

icnelia
"To help or benefit someone, to favor them, to befriend them." This term comes as close as any in Nahuatl to the English contemporary sense of altruism.

ihuiyan, icemel
"Peacefully." "Calmly." Together, they form *difrasismo* for tranquility, though not as an end goal, as the ancient Greek and Roman Skeptics thought of *ataraxia*, but as a manner of conducting oneself in the presence of others. The opposite of *ihuiyan*—namely, *aihuiyan*—is typically translated as "disturbed."

ilhuilli
"Merit, due, compensation." The translation typically renders it as "due."

imati "To be careful in what one does. To be deft, to know how to do something well, to be expert in something." Philosophically, this term functions as a kind of wisdom in knowing how to do something where this sort of knowledge is gained by having done it many times previously.

ixco, icpac "On the face, on the surface, before one." "Above, over, on top." Together, they form a *difrasismo* that in most context means lacking respect. It is a person who puts themselves before others or above them in their concerns.

ixtli, yollotl "Face or eye." "Heart, life, spirits." Together they form a *difrasismo* for the core of a person, their character in an ethical sense. There has been a significant scholarly debate whether *ixtli* meant "face" or "eye" primarily, but for ethical purposes "face" in the sense of one's visage proves more apt. The translation thus circumvents that debate.

ixtomahuac "Someone simple, an imbecile." Of things, it means that they are "dense or thick." The root terms are *ixtli* and *tomahuac*. In ethical contexts, this compound term is used to discuss a person who lacks prudence.

macehua "To obtain or deserve a thing." This is a way of expressing deserts and so is related to a conception of justice as fairness. A commoner is called a *mecehualli*, and that may bear relation to the object noun *macehualli* derived from the verb. A *macehualli* was also a human being. The possible etymological connection might suggest dependence of commoners or humans on something greater.

nantli, tatli   "Mother." "Father." Together they form a *difrasismo* that often indicates the leader of the *altepetl* (city) who watches out for the commoners (*macehualli*) as parents would.

-nehuiyan   This is a necessarily possessed term meaning "oneself," "one's own," or "personally." It does not involve a concept of will, even though using that term might make a translation more idiomatic. The translation avoided "will" because that notion proves important in "Western" philosophy but has no obvious analog in Nahua thought.

nemactli   "One's inheritance; grant, gift, endowment; merit; fortune or lot; spouse." The translation typically uses "one's lot in life."

ohtli, xopechtli   The first of these means a "road or way"; the second a "foundation." These are not a *difrasismo* since the terms are used independently in many contexts. In paragraph 8, they are used in a mutually reinforcing way as the path of one's life (*ohtli*) and the principle that guides one's life (*xopechtli*).

ompa   Meaning "there, over there" in a locative sense, or "then" temporally. In the present work, its meaning as "then" shades into "in that case." It appears, in short, to function modally.

paqui   "To be or become happy" in the sense of experiencing pleasure or elevated emotional states. It may also mean to enjoy oneself.

petlatl, icpalli   "Reed mat." "The seat," in the sense that it is a seat of authority. This is a *difrasismo* meaning not only the throne of a *tlahtoani*, a "king," but the broader domain of rulership and authority.

quauhtli, ocelotl   "Eagle." "Jaguar" (*felis onca*) or "ocelot" (*felis pardalis*). As a *difrasismo* it means a warrior, but also serves as a metaphor for courage, the thing that warriors do. It may also refer to their regalia or status. Notably, Olmos also records *quauhyotl* independently as "bravery."

temoxtli, ehecatl   This is a *difrasismo* for pestilence. *Ehecatl* is "wind," but the meaning of *temoxtli*, used in isolation, is not known.

tetl, quahuitl   "Stone." "Wood." This is a *difrasismo* referring to the way that people are punished, but in ethical contexts it tends to mean consequences.

teutli, tlazolli   "Dust." "Trash, dirt, filth." This appears to be a contact-era *difrasismo* used by Catholic clergymen to communicate what is sinful. In Nahua thought, what was dusty or filthy would be balanced out with activities of "purification" and literal cleaning. And the use to which the clergymen put it appears to reflect their own views on sexuality.

tlacatecolotl   "The owlman." A not well understood figure from Nahua culture who appears to have done malicious things using mysterious powers. During the early contact era, Church fathers used his connection with danger to take the place of devils or Satan.

tlacuilolli,
machiyotl,
tlapaltzintli

"Document, painting, anything written." "Signal, sign, pattern, model, paradigm." "Paint, dye, color, red." In this work the terms appear together as part of an extended metaphor, something close to a *difrasismo*, meaning, in the first case, what is written down. A more common expression uses *tlilli, tlapalli*, meaning "the black ink, the red ink." In a slightly more metaphorical sense, what is at stake concerns the wisdom which is written and passed down through tradition. Such matters include both theoretical and practical wisdom.

tlahtolli

"A word, thought, idea, or notion." Also written *tlatolli*. It is unexpectedly close to the Greek *logos* and can likewise range from a literal word to a thought, to an entire doctrine or teaching.

tlalticpac

"On the earth, on the ground; the world." This is opposed to *"cemanahuac,"* which is the earth or world in the sense of the conjunction of everything that is near. When used existentially, *tlalticpac* indicates our human position as below the heavens and above what is under the earth, which is why it has a specifically locative construction. When used in an ethical context it means the set of circumstances that condition our pursuit of the good life. These circumstances are said to be "slippery," meaning not only that we are prone to fail, but that even good lives fall into error at some point. For the Nahuas, moral luck forms a permanent feature of our condition.

tlatlacolli   "A sin, fault, defect, wrong deed, error." The term is formed from the verb *ihtlacoa*, meaning either "to become spoiled" or "to damage something or someone." The moral notion, then, is a wrong. The clergymen of the colonial era tried to press the world into the meaning of "sin," just as the Christian Bible, in Koine Greek, pressed the term *hamartia*, meaning "an error," into "sin."

tlazotla   This term means "to love, esteem, or treat another person well." Its derivational base, from the element *tlazoh-*, is used in terms to mean "to value, love, or feel affection." To some degree, it approximates the Greek *axiō*, which turns on the activities of esteeming or valuing, though not loving.

tleyotl, mahuizotl   "Honor, fame." "The honor or high status of the elite." This is a *difrasismo* for an excellent reputation. This was thought to be both a good and part of a life well lived—one which observes its social duties well. It is explicitly linked to the middle way (*nepantla*) needed for living within a community (see par. 43).

tlilli, tlapalli   "Black ink." "Red ink." This is a *difrasismo* for what is written down in these inks. The metaphorical notion in these contexts extends to a sense of wisdom, both theoretical and practical.

tolinia   "To be poor, afflicted, bothered, in need of attention, to suffer." In the ethical context of these *Discourses*, it tends to range between suffering and lacking tranquility, and so proves difficult to translate consistently.

yectli   "Something good." "Something pure, clean." The intransitive verb means to make oneself better, to put oneself in order. The transitive verb means to clean or purify something else. The applicative (which adds an extra object, often translated as an indirect object in English) means to justify or provide a defense for another. One abstractive verbal form, *yectiliztli*, is even given the sense of goodness, justice, and virtue by Siméon (1977). The translation has typically preferred to use "right" when possible, but implied in the notion is something along the lines of "rectitude," so that "straight" often proved more apt in the later Christian paragraphs.

yollotia   "To inspire someone to do something." Used reflexively and in combination with a good teaching, a *tlahtolli*, as *ti-c-mo-yollotia*, meaning "to *enheart* the teaching." This is one of the metaphors used for habituation.

References

Adamson, Peter. 2014. *Classical Philosophy: A History of Philosophy without Any Gaps.* Oxford: Oxford University Press.

Andrews, J. Richard. 2003. *Introduction to Classical Nahuatl.* Norman: University of Oklahoma Press.

Aristotle. *Ethica Nicomachae.* 1894. Edited and annotated by I. Bywater. Oxford: Oxford University Press.

Aristotle. *Aristotelis Metaphysica.* 1957. Edited and annotated by W. Jaeger. Oxford: Oxford University Press.

Bierhorst, John. 1985. *Cantares Mexicanos: Songs of the Aztecs.* Stanford: Stanford University Press.

Burkhart, Louise. 1989. *The Slippery Earth: Nahua-Christian Moral Dialogue in Sixteenth-Century Mexico.* Tucson: University of Arizona Press.

Codex Chimalpopoca: Text in Nahuatl with a Glossary and Grammatical Notes. 1992. Transcribed by John Bierhorst. Tuscon: University of Arizona Press.

Crisp, Roger. 2008. *Reasons and the Good.* Oxford: Oxford University Press.

Dodds Pennock, Caroline. 2008. *Bonds of Blood: Gender, Lifecycle and Sacrifice in Aztec Culture.* New York: Palgrave Macmillan.

Durán, Diego. 1967. *Historia de las Indias de Nueva España e islas de la tierra firme.* 2 vols. Edited by Angel María Garibay K. Mexico City: Editorial Porrúa.

Furst, Jill Leslie McKeever. 1995. *The Natural History of the Soul in Ancient Mexico.* New Haven: Yale University Press.

García Quintana, Josefina. 1974. "Exhortación de un padre a su hijo, texto recopilado por Andrés de Olmos." *Estudios de Cultura Náhuatl* (Universidad Nacional Autónoma de México, Instituto de Investigaciones Históricas) 11: 137–82.

———. 1976. "El huehuetlahtolli, antigua palabra, como fuente para la historia sociocultural de los nahuas." *Estudios de Cultura Náhuatl* (Universidad Nacional Autónoma de México, Instituto de Investigaciones Históricas) 12: 61–70.

Garibay K., Ángel María. (1953–1954) 2007. *Historia de la literatura Náhuatl*. 2 vols. Mexico City: Porrúa Press.

Homer. 1917. *Odyssaea* in *Homeri Opera*. Vols. 3–4. Edited and annotated by Thomas W. Allen. Oxford: Oxford University Press.

———. 1967. *The Odyssey: A New Verse Translation*. Translated by Albert Cook. New York: W. W. Norton.

Hursthouse, Rosalind. 1999. *On Virtue Ethics*. Oxford: Oxford University Press.

Irwin, Terence. 2020. *Ethics through History: An Introduction*. Oxford: Oxford University Press.

Ixtlilxóchitl, Fernando Alva De. 1891. *Obras Históricas de Don Fernando de Alva Ixtlilxochitl*. Vols. 1–2. Annotated by Alfredo Chavero. Mexico City: Oficina de la secretaria de fomento.

Jordan, Mark. 1997. *The Invention of Sodomy in Christian Theology*. Chicago: University of Chicago Press.

Kant, Immanuel. 1987. *Critique of Judgement*. Translated by Werner S. Pluhar. Indianapolis: Hackett.

Karttunen, Frances. 1983. *An Analytical Dictionary of Nahuatl*. Norman: University of Oklahoma Press.

Launey, Michel. 2004. "The Features of Omnipredicativity in Classical Nahuatl." *Sprachtypologie und Universalienforschung* 57: 49–69.

León-Portilla, Miguel. (1956) 1993. *La filosofía náhuatl: Estudiada en sus fuentes*. Mexico City: Instituto de Investigaciones Antropológicas UNAM.

———. 1996. *El destino de la palabra*. Mexico City: Fondo de Cultura Económica.

Lockhart, James. 1992. *The Nahuas after the Conquest: A Social and Cultural History of the Indians of Central Mexico, Sixteenth through Eighteenth Centuries*. Stanford, Calif.: Stanford University Press.

López Austin, Alfredo. 1967. "Cuarenta clases de magos del mundo náhuatl." *Estudios de Cultura Náhuatl*, vol. 7: 87–117.

———. (1980) 2004. *Cuerpo humano e ideología: Las concepciones de los antiguos nahuas*. 2 vols. Mexico City: Instituto de Investigaciones Antropológicas UNAM.

———. 2015. "Sobre el concepto de cosmovisión" in *Cosmovisión mesoamericana: Reflex-*

iones, polémicas y etnografías. Edited by Alejandra Gámez Espinosa and Alfredo López Austin. Mexico City: Fondo de Cultura Económica.

Lucretius. 1977. *On the Nature of Things*. Translated by Frank Copley. New York: W. W. Norton.

Maffie, James. 2014. *Aztec Philosophy: Understanding a World in Motion*. Boulder: University of Colorado Press.

McLeod, Alexus. 2018. *Philosophy of the Ancient Maya*. Lanham, Md.: Lexington Books.

Mendieta, Gerónimo de. (1945) 1980. *Historia eclesiástica indiana: Obra escrita a fines del siglo XVI*. Mexico City: Editorial Porrúa.

Mignolo, Walter. 2005. *The Idea of Latin America*. Malden, MA: Blackwell.

Molina, Alonso de. 2001. *Vocabulario en lengua castellana y Mexicana y mexicana y castellana*, 4th ed. Facsimile of 1571 edition. Mexico City: Porrúa.

Nāgārjuna. 1995. *The Fundamental Wisdom of the Middle Way: Nāgārjuna's Mūlamadhyamakakārikā*. Translated by Jay L. Garfield. New York: Oxford University Press.

Olmos, Andrés de. 1991. *Huehuetlahtolli: Testimonios de la antigua palabra*. Recorded by Andrés de Olmos. Transliterated and translated into Spanish by Librado Silva Galeana. Mexico City: Fondo de Cultura Económica.

Paz, Octavio. 2014. *Los privilegios de la vista, Arte moderno universal, Arte de México*. Volume 4 of *Octavio Paz: Obras Completas*. Mexico City: Fondo de Cultura Económica.

Plato. 1968. *The Republic of Plato*. Translated by Allan Bloom. New York: Basic Books.

———. 1995. "*Apologia Socratis*" in *Platonis Opera*, vol. 1. Edited and annotated by E. A. Duke, W. S. M. Nicoll, and D. B. Robinson. Oxford: Oxford Classical Texts.

———. 2003. *Platonis Respvblicam*. Edited and annotated by S. R. Slings. Oxford: Oxford Classical Texts.

Popul Vuh: Literal Poetic Version. 2007. Translated and transcribed by Allen J. Christenson. Norman: University of Oklahoma Press.

The Popul Vuh: A New English Version. 2018. Translated by Michael Bazzett. Minneapolis: Seedbank.

Popul Vuh: The Sacred Book of the Maya. 2003. Translated by Allen J. Christenson. Norman: University of Oklahoma Press.

Purcell, L. Sebastian. 2017. "*Eudaimonia* and *Neltiliztli*: Aristotle and the Aztecs on the Good Life." *American Philosophical Association Newsletter on Hispanic/Latino Issues* 16: 10–21.

———. 2018. "On What There 'Is': Aristotle and the Aztecs on Being and Existence." *American Philosophical Association Newsletter on Native American and Indigenous Philosophy* 18: 11–23.

———. 2020. "Hermeneutic, Comparative, Syncretic Philosophy, or, on Ricoeurian, Confucian, and Aztec Philosophy." *Journal of French and Francophone Philosophy* 28: 46–69.

———. 2021. "Truth, Rootedness, and the Good Life in Aztec Ethical Philosophy." *American Philosophical Association Newsletter on Native American and Indigenous Philosophy* 21: 4–11.

Quine, Willard Van Orman. 1980. *From a Logical Point of View: Nine Logico-Philosophical Essays.* Cambridge: Harvard University Press.

Radin, Paul. (1927) 2017. *Primitive Man as Philosopher.* New York: New York Review of Books.

Restall, Matthew. 2018. *When Montezuma Met Cortez.* New York: HarperCollins.

Russell, Daniel. 2009. *Practical Intelligence and the Virtues.* Oxford: Oxford University Press.

Sahagún, Bernardino de. 1953–1982. *Florentine Codex: General History of the Things of New Spain.* 13 vols. Edited and translated by Arthur J. O. Anderson and Charles E. Dibble. Santa Fe: School of American Research and the University of Utah.

———. 1956. *Historia de las cosas de Nueva España.* Edited by Ángel María Garibay K. Mexico City: Editorial Porrúa.

———. *Historia de las cosas de Nueva España: Códice Matritense de la Real Academia.* Digital edition available at http://bdmx.mx/documento/bernardino-sahagun-codices-matritenses.

———. 1997. *Primeros Memoriales: Paleography of Nahuatl Text and English Translation.* Translated by Thelma D. Sullivan. Norman: University of Oklahoma Press.

Santana, Alejandro. 2008. *American Philosophical Association Newsletter on Hispanic/ Latino Issues in Philosophy,* vol. 8: 2–9.

Seler, Eduard. (1904) 1963. *Comentarios al Códice Borgia.* Mexico City: Fondo de Cultura Económica.

Sigal, Pete. 2011. *The Flower and the Scorpion: Sexuality and Ritual in Early Nahua Culture.* Durham: Duke University Press.

Siméon, Rémi. 1977. *Diccionario de la lenga Nahuatl o mexicana redactado según los documentos impresos y manuscritos más auténticos y precedido de una introducción.* Translated by Josefina Oliva de Coll. Mexico City: Siglo Veintiuno. Original French edition, 1885.

Soustelle, Jacques. 1955. *La vie quotidienne des aztèques à la vielle de la conquête espagnole.* Paris: Hachette.

van Norden, Bryan. 2017. *Taking Back Philosophy: A Multicultural Manifesto.* New York: Columbia University Press.

Whitehead, Alfred North. 1978. *Process and Reality.* Edited by David Ray Griffin and Donald W. Sherburne. New York: Free Press.

Index